SRI CHAITANYADEV AND SRI GADADHAR

SRI CHAITANYADEV AND SRI GADADHAR

RADHAKRISHNA GOSWAMI

KALPAZ

Sri Chaitanyadev and Sri Gadadhar

Rs. 540

ISBN: 978-81-7835-771-3

Published in 2010 in India by
Kalpaz Publications
C-30, Satyawati Nagar,
Delhi-110052
E-mail: kalpaz@hotmail.com
Phone : 9212729499

Lasser Type Setting by: Quick Media, Delhi
Printed at : GIAN RIDHI OFFSET PRINTERS

To
my Daughter
Mandira Ganguly
and
Esha Goswami Anwesha Goswami
Kshama Bhattacharya and
Seema Bhattacharya

CONTENTS

PREFACE

बंदे गुरुनीशभक्तानीशमीशबतारकान।
तत् प्रकाशंश्च तत्शक्तिः कृष्णाचैतन्य संगकम्॥ (In Sanskrit)

Bande Gurunishbhaktanishaavatarkan
Tatprakashangashcha Tatchchhaktih Krishnachaitanyasangakam

At first I bow to the Preceptors (of Diksha and Siksha), the Devotees of God (Sri Baas and Others), the Incarnation of God (Sri Adyaitacharya and Others), Publicisers of God (Sri Nityananda and Others), Strength of God (Sri Gadadhar and Others) and God-Lord Sri Krishna named Sri Krishna Chaitanyadev.

Introduction

500 years back the geopolitical stereotype of Bengal was different than it is of today. The social scenario was severe, if it is in financial sector, in agriculture, in basic education or in healthcare sector Bengal lagged behind, in addition to that it suffered draught, floods and famines too. Not only that epidemics, communal riots and invasions were other problems that cornered Bengal to the extreme darkness.

Sad but it is true that in Bengal, like in other places of India, Brahmin and upper class people enjoyed right to oppress the lower class people. They called it Samaj (society). People who used to run this Samaj behaved like local monarchs, if they thought any person crossed Samaj-set regulations they used to jump in to impose social sanctions.

Suffocated Bengal was dying for fresh air.

500 years back a man emerged, he changed the scene, he did it with love, wiped out boundaries set by so called samaj, this new king created a new samaj for lovers. He is the all time Hero Sri Chaitanya Dev, and he was accompanied by Sri Gadadhar Pundit.

Usually people know little about Gadadhar. All along he stayed with Mahaprabhu from childhood to the last hours of Holly Disappearances. Here through this Chaitanya Biography I have also tried my best to portray this character before my learned readers.

To do so I have a great debt to the historical connotations and references given by scholars of Vaishnavism cult.

Radhakrishna Goswami (Radhu Goswami)

Date : / /2009

68, NABARUNPALLI, SODEPUR, KOLKATA-700110

ACKNOWLEDGEMENTS

The author expresses the indebtedness to many books and persons specially the undenoted—

1. Sri Chaitanya Bhagawat by Vrindavandas (Reflect Publication),
2. Sri Sri Chaitanya Charitamrita by Krishnadas Kabiraj (Reflect Publication),
3. Baangaali Charitabhidhan by Sahitya Samsad Publication (4th Ed. Part-1),
4. Baangaali Manishay Sri Chaitanya-Ed. Nirmalnarayan Gupta,
5. Sri Sri Chaitanyadev by Swami Sardeshananda (Udbodhan),
6. Chaitnyadev: Etihaas O Abadan - Dilip Kumar Biswas (Ed. Avantikumar Sannyal O Ashoke Bhattacharya),
7. Amritava by Navin Chandra Sen,
8. Sri Chaitanya Mangal by Lochandas (Ed. Kishoridas Babaji),
9. Goudiya Tirtha Paryatan by Kishoridas Babaji,
10. Prachin Banga Sahitya by Kalidas Roy,

11. Gour Gadadhar Lila by with Srila Mukundalal Goswami, Bhakti Siroman
12. Sukhendu Baur in Smaranika ('Praktani' ed. A. Kundu CU ex. Beng Dpt.),
13. Akhanda Amiya Sri Gouranga-Achintakumar Sengupta,
14. Various Songs and Gora by Rabindranath Tagore,
15. Sri Amiya Nemai Charit by Mahatma Sisir Kumar Ghose,
16. Sahitya Mela-Ed. Purnenduprasad Bhattacharya,
17. Sadhak Jiban Charit by Ganesh Chandra Mukhopadhyay,
18. Virangana by Michael Madhusudan Dutta,
19. Sri Chaitanya O Sri Ramkrishna by Bramhachari Akshoy Chaitanya,
20. Goudiya Vaishnav Darshaner Bhumika - Sri Chaitanyadev O Bhaktidharma by Dr. Skhendu Sekhar Gangopadhyay,
21. Vaishnav Dharma O Darshan by Dr. Biswanath Roy (as above 12),
22. Chaitanya Jiban Katha by Bijitkumar Dutta,
23. Dr. Asit Kumar Bandyopadhyay in preface of above 20,
24. Sri Sri Shikshastakam by Srimad Anantadas Babaji Maharaj of Radhakunda, Mathura,
25. Amiya Vaisnav Sadhana by Harekrishna Mukhopadhyay,
26. Chaitanya Parikrama - Bharatiya Sanskritir Roopakar Sri Chaitanya by Prasit Roychowdhury,

27. Sadhanananda Mishra in Viswa Hindu Barta (in 500 years' of Sri Chaitatanya birth),
28. Bangalee Manishay Sri Chaitanya - (as above 4) wrote Biman Behari Majumdar,
29. Dr. Hansanarayan Bhattacharya (as above in 27),
30. Sri Chaitanya Ananta Jibaner Satyanweshan by Durgapada Chattopadhyay,
31. Sri Sri Bhaktamal by Krishnadas Babaji (the Basumati Publication in 464 Chaitanyabada),
32. Bharatiya Darshanprasthaney Vaishnav Sadhanar Dhara by Dr. Sudhir Ranjan Chattopadhyay (Burdwan University),
33. Manab Premik Nityananda - Dr. Uma Bandyopadhyay,
34. Mahaprabhu'r Krishna Avisaar by Sri Madhusudan
35. Srimad Bhagawat (by the author Xth Scandha Haraf Prakashani, then run by Abdul Aziz Aal Aaman Kolkata and Gita Press, Gorakhpur).
36. Acharya Srila Pran Kishore Goswami, M.A., Bhagwatacharya.
37. Prabhupad Bijan Behari Goswami, M.A., Dip-in-Lib, Kavya-Vyakaran-Vaishnav Darshan-Vedanta Tirtha, Bhagwat Shastri.
38. Apurba Kumar Saha, Jagari (ed.)
39. Smt. Bhumika Goswami.
40. Shri Hindol Goswami.
41. Shri Anindya Goswami.
42. Shri Naresh Chandra Sarkar

1
LOVE

God is Love and Love is God. Mahaprabhu Sri Chaitanyadev taught us that love to human being is the urgent part of love to God. If someone loves God, he can love others, if he can love all in the Universe he can love God. The religion of love was the main theme of Lord Sri Chaitanyadev. He had madly love for Sri Krishna, Sri Krishna is the Satchidananda Bigraha Param Purusha.

Almost the same theme echoed in many voices of the world. We find that the renowned philosopher and once the honourable President of India Dr. S. Radhakrishnan wrote in his Religion and Society-"Through love we create a spiritual reality. The tempest of the heart are taken over into the calm of the soul. Love is not merely flame but spirit calling to spirit". He in his S. Eastern Religions and Western Thought has also written-"Nothing human is alien to us. We are no more members of this or that particular group, belong to humanity as a whole". Again,"In fact, today what needs is not much more Hinduism but its glowing vision of mankind as a family-Vasudhaiva Kutumbakam'."

Respect for Mankind

Respect all, consider everybody equal, all are human beings; this is what concisely Sri Gourangadev (after sannyas named Sri Krishna Chaitanya or Sri Chaitanyadev) taught Bengal as well as all of the world.

Once He proclaimed that Chandal might be more acceptable if he pronounces the name of Lord Sri Krishna than a dishonest Brahmin. He realized that the caste system made the society crippled. Therefore, His intention was to wipe it out. He wanted to obliterate differences in between people, not only in Bengal but also in the whole country, so He traveled off the beaten path of India on bare feet, lonely, chanting Krishnanam, from north to south and to the remotest place of the East.

Adwyaitacharya

Before the divine birth of Sri Gouranga Mahaprabhu middle aged pious Kamalaksha Bhattacharya widely known as Sri Adwyaitacharya (1434-1558) observed prolonged disorder in the society. He was expecting that Lord Sri Krishna should reappear on this earth to protect the lives of the innocents and to drive out the mischief from the society as He assured in the Srimadbhagwatgita (the Gita). He worshipped Lord Sri Krishna with His favouriteTulsi leaves along with water of the holy river Ganga and prayed to Him to reappear in the world in order to establish peace. Older Adwyaitacharya was eagerly waiting for reappearance of God, 'Krishnastubhagawanswyam' Sri Krishna who always saves and will save the Creations from all kinds of odds in the Universe.

Worshipping Lord Sri Krishna in Nabadwip

A handful people only used to worship Lord Sri Krishna in Nabadwip and in whole Bengal. Worshipping of the goddesses of Power and Strength and Lord Shiva Mahadeva was in practice. However, most of the worshippers of Shakti and common men used to consume huge amount of liquor, meat etc. and indulged many other types of ill habits in the name of worshiping the goddess in many names. People forgot their culture. Most of them were satisfied with the present lifestyle. Hardly one thought for the future, art, education and literature. None considered to get prepared oneself to protect from the hands of tyranny and oppression from the then society and political adverse situations. Rather, their ill motivated habits would tend to effect on the innocent, pious and peace loving people. People had also to forget any other kind of amusement. Sometime people hardly dared to think that they are also human beings and they have the right to live peacefully in own land.

The Divine Birth

On the day of Holi Festival Sri Chaitanyadev was born in the lap of Mother Sachidevi. Father was Jagannath (Purandar) Mishra.

The Holi Festival known as Dolyatra (festival of Sri Krishna's giving colours to Gopis and others). People of the whole Country chant songs on God in Holi (on the day of full moon) festival. That evening was of lunar eclipse and it was visible from Nabadwip. Nabadwip was full of chanting for Lord Sri Krishna. Otherwise, hardly people cared for the name of Lord Sri Krishna. The season was spring so the environment was full of various colourful flowers and green leaves with sweet breeze.

According to Vrindavandas, He was born during lunar eclipse but many scholars differed and have said that after the Divine Birth the lunar eclipse started at about 8 p.m. but Mahaprabhu was born in the evening before the eclipse started.

On Saturday (as also confirmed and written by Dr. Biman Behari Majumdar in Srichaitanya Chariter Aba daan) 22/23 Falguna 1407 Saka i.e. 18/19 February (as per Julian Calendar) or was 27 February (as per Gregorian Calendar) in 1486 A.D. Mahaprabhu was born.

Sri Chaitanyadev was fair in complexion so He was named as Gour (fair) Anga (body) i.e. Gouranga, in short Gour. His mother Sachidevi and the neighbourers called Him 'Nemai' in nickname as Gouranga was born in a hut under a Neem (margosa) tree. Moreover, among her eight issues six daughters did not survive. Therefore, in similar cases mothers in the society are fond of giving name a son in the name of some bitter thing so that the god of death Jomraj does not prefer to look at a bitter thing. Thus, a mother thinks the issue will survive by averting death.

Mahaprabhu's other name was Vishwambhar in tune of his elder brother's name Vishwarup.

On Sannyas Keshav Bharati, the Preceptor of Sannyas, at Katwa awarded Mahaprabhu Sri Gourangadev the name "Sri Krishnachaitanya".

The Five Pioneers - Panchatattwa

Devotees prefer to worship the great five pioneers of Goudiya Vaishnav Movement. The Panchatattwa comprises of Lord Sri Gouranga, Sri Gadadhar, Sri Nityananda, Sri Adwyaitacharya and Sri Baas. This is Panchatattwa.

Sri Gourangadev's main associate was Sri Gadadhar Pundit. He was a lifelong partner of Mahaprabhu. He was one and half month's junior and in innocent like look with amiable nature. Gadadhar from his childhood used to worship Lord Sri Krishna as his parents Madhab Mishra and Ratnadevi were disciples of eminent Vaishnav Madhabendra Puri. Sri Gadadhar Pundit was the power of God. He was considered as Radha, the hladini shakti of Lord Sri Krishna.

Next was Sri Adwyaitacharya who was 52 yrs' older than Mahaprabhu. He welcomed the Sri Chaitanya's appearance in spreading the name of Hari, the Lord Sri KRISHNA and led Gouranga Mahaprabhu to go ahead. Sri Adwyaitacharya was considered as incarnation of God Shiva Mahadeva.

Sri Baas with all the members of his family was also an important devotee and provided his dwelling house in

Nabadwip for Hari Samkirtan organized by Sri Gouranga Mahaprabhu. Sri Baas was a pure devotee of Lord Sri Krishna.

Significant inclusion was prabhu Nityananda, twelve years' older a strong built feature with varied knowledge and experience acquired by roaming throughout India from his twelve to thirtytwo. While Gouranga Mahaprabhu started the movement with associates at Sri Baas angan Nityananda joined the team and stood at the side of Mahaprabhu. Nityananda Prabhu was as Balaram.

Other Close Associates

More above Adwyaitacharya, Gadadhar, Nityananda, Sri Baas others who made the team of Samkirtan was Haridas, importantly the unconditional devotee of Lord Sri Krishna and known as Yaban Haridas. In addition who at initial stage gave their full support to Gouranga Mahaprabhu were Sanjay, Mukunda, Chandrasekhar, Suklambar Brahmachari, Sridhar, Pundarik Vidyanidhi, first Preceptor of Gouranga Mahaprabhu Ishwar Puri, second and Sannyas Preceptor Keshab Bharati, changed Jagai-Madhai.

Otherswere

Swarup Damodar, Roy Ramanada, Sarbobhoum Acharya, Jagadananda, Buddhimanta Khan, Narayan, Kashiswar, Basudev Ghose, Ram Garurai, Gobinda, Sadashiv, Sriman, Gobindananda, Jagadish, Bakreswar,

Srigarva, Jayananda, Ragav Pundit, Makardhwaj, Purushottam, Ram, Gopinath, Krishnananda, Brahmananda, Paramananda Puri, Purushananda, Pradyumna Mishra, Premananda, Pradyumna Brahmachari, Damodar Pandit, Srisankar Pundit, Bhagawan Acharya, Kashi Mishra at whose house Mahaprabhu remained in Puri, Janardan, Murari Mahiti, Sikhi Mahiti, Murari Mishra, Vishnudas, Praharaj Mahapatra, Paramananda Mahapatra, Bhabananda Roy (father of Roy Ramananda), Baninath Patnaik (brother of Roy Ramanada), Rambhadracharya, Chhoto Haridas, Purandar Pundit, Gopal Bhatta, Ballav Bhatta (disciple of Gadadhar and some say as Ballavacharya), Roop Goswami, Sanatan Goswami, Srijib Goswami, Achyutananda (son of Adwyaitacharya and disciple of Gadadhar), Lokenath Goswami, Ballav Chaitanya Goswami, Bhugarva, Raghunathdas, Das Gadadhar, Ramdas, Krishnadas Pundit and more others including the then the King of Orissa Maharaja Pratap Rudra joined with Lord Sri Chaitanyadev. They all and many others served for Lord Sri Krishna and gave their complete support to Chaitanya Mahaprabhu in Nabadwip and Neelachal and also in Vrindavan-Mathura.

Six Goswamis

The followers in Neelachal, in whole of Bengal and in Vrindavan all were engaged to chalk out and maintain the Vaishnav rites and rules according to Vaishnav Philosophy as directed and discussed by Sri Chaitanyadev from time to time.

In Vrindavan there were six Goswamis mainly who took the part of mammoth work of writing books on Goudiya Vaishnavism. They were Sri Sanatan, Sri Roop, Sri Raghunath Bhatta, Sri Gopal Bhatta, Sri Jib, Sri Raghunathdas and more other two were there as among the Six Goswamis were Sri Bhugarva and Sri Lokenath Goswami.

Sri Jib Goswami was son of Anupam one of the three brothers Sri Sanatan and Sri Roop Goswami. Anupam had premature death.

Essence of Goudiya Vaishnavism

From the dawn of this Earth, we find Brahma as a Vaishnava. Shiva Mahadeva was also a Vaishnava. From the collection from excavations at different places in undivided India, the deities, utensils, weapons, etc. as used by the people of ancient ages we can know or guess our past. Importantly among other things many deities of Sri Vishnu were discovered.

The very word 'Vaishnav' is available in the great Mahabharata. It has also evidence that the eighteen Puaranas were composed before writing of the Mahabharata as those are referred to in the great epic.

Vaishnav means the worshipper of Lord Vishnu. In Panini's Astadhyai written 700 B.C., we can find the word Vasudevak that expresses worshipper of Lord Vishnu. This Vasudevak and the religion of Bhagwata probably existed long before 7th century B.C.

The rulers of the Gupta dynasty used to introduce themselves as Param Bhagawata. In the Rig Veda with 'Idang Vishnurvichakrame' the sages prayed to Vishnu 'Vishno Sumating Bhajammahe'.

In the Yajurveda this Vishnu is described the Yagnapurusha.

In the Oiteraya Brahman Vishnu has been described the Supreme-'Vishnurparama' and 'Devanam Dwaparah' i.e. all gods and goddesses are worshipped at His door.

Even in the Srimad Bhagwatgita, known as the Gita, Lord Sri Krishna advised Arjuna-

"Ahang Hi Sarbayagnang Bhokta cha Prabhureb cha,

Na Tu Mamabhijananti Tattwenatashchyabanti Te." (9/24)

I am the ultimate receiver and the Lord of all the things that offered to any gods but no one can apprehend the reality of mine.

In the Gita (9/32) Lord Sri Krishna assured Partha that anybody born anywhere, in any caste irrespective of any religions who worships Me, the Ultimate, gets supreme celestial position.

Vasudeva-Vishnu-Narayana is the same and the One as per the Gita.

In the Taittariya Aranyaka-

"Narayana Bidmahe, Basudevaya Dhimahi, Tanno Vishnuh Prachodayat"- I know Narayana, I meditate to

Him as Vasudeva, He is Vishnu, He is the Almighty and directs everything in the Universe.

Lord Sri Krishna in the Gita said to Arjuna also—

'Brishninam Vasudevohashmi'.

In the explanation by the Patanjal we find—'Asadhurmatule Krishnah ebang Jaghan Kansam Kil Vasudevah'.

Lord Gourangadev of Nabadwip became overwhelmed with the Love for Lord Sri Krishna. Sri Gourangadev established the Goudiya Vaishnavism through His followers and scriptures composed by many followers at Vrindavan, Srikshetra (Neelachal), Nabadwip, and some other places.

The thoughts were on social lives and religious simplicity so that the mere illiterate people almost living below the poverty line and socially deprived of human prestige may breathe on this earth easily like other people living on the high altitude with intellect, money and prestigious position. And the people of high altitude also can find easy entrance into Vaishnavism. Once Sri Chaitanyadev said wherever you are born that is not to be judged but you must remain honest to yourself and pronounce the name of Lord Sri Krishna. Whoever once utters the name of Lord Sri Krishna he is welcomed, but having born in the high families if one remains dishonest or does not utter the name of Lord Sri Krishna in ones lips is cursed. Mahaprabhu Sri Chaitanyadev tried to remind all to think themselves as man, as human being with values because God makes all creatures in the Universe and He remains in all creations. Therefore, Vaishnavism welcomes everyone of this earth to live in peace and harmony by leaving aside all the differences still we find here and there in the world.

Some Writers on the Holy Life

The familiar writers on the divine life of Sri Chaitanyadev were Vrindavandas, son of Narayani-Baikuntha and disciple of Prabhu Nityananda (Sri Chaitanya Bhagawata), Krishnadas Kaviraj (Sri Sri Chaitanyacharitamrita), Murari Gupta (Karcha), Lochandas (Sri Chaitanyamangal), Kavi Karnapur (Sri Chaitanyacharitamrita Mahakavya and Chaitanyachandrodaya drama), Sri Sanatan-Sri Roop-Sri Jib Goswami, Prabodhananda Saraswati and Raghunathdas Goswami.

Writers on the topic of Holy Life of Sri Chaitanyadev, His works, Philosophy were hundreds during the 500 years and till date. They were Basudev Ghosh, Pradyumna Mishra and many others in Bengal, Odissa, Vrindavan and all over the world. All received blessings directly or indirectly from Sri Chaitanyadev. We are indebted to them and the writers of the last one or two centuries like Mahatma Sisir Kumar Ghose, Navin Chandra Sen, Dr. Mahanambrata Brahmachari, Acharya Prankishore Goswami, Mukundalal Goswami and many hundreds others who took the responsibility voluntarily to pubicise Harinaam Movement and the holy life of Sri Chaitanyadev with the associates and His philosophy among us.

2

SRI GOURANGADEV IN THE CHILDHOOD

'Nemai' in the childhood like other children was fond of playing, going outside to see the surprises of the vast world. Once, some thieves found him unguarded with precious gold ornaments on his body. One of them took him in his lap and then on shoulder as if carrying own son. They started to walk. However, taking him, they roamed here and there for a long time and at last, they reached near the house of Jagannath Mishra at the same place from where they took him. The thieves could not succeed to steal the ornaments. Vaishnavite people believe that the thieves were also blessed as they carried God on their shoulders. Once He played with a snake also and lay asleep on it.

Once an ascetic came to the house of Jagannath Mishra and he was offered materials to cook, as he was a self-cook, for preparation food for his worshipped Shalagram as Lord Sri Krishna. The ascetic cooked and offered food to his Shalagram. On the other hand, little Gouranga thought the ascetic called him to take the food. Gour with beautiful red eyes, nice feet to look, dust on his body came to the place and started to take the food. The ascetic's efforts, as he thought, thus became scraps.

Again, on request of Jagannath Mishra, after necessary rebuking the child Nemai, the strict disciplined and sincere ascetic cooked and in the same way, Gour spoiled it. The child innocently gave plea that the pious man called him from his heart, so he could not resist himself of coming over the place. Third time there reached Vishwarup with godly appearance having sacred thread on his shoulder.

The guest ascetic became much pleased to see Vishwarup the elder brother of Gouranga. Both of them greeted each other with due respect. On his earnest request the sage told him that God has not written food for him so fruits etc as available at home will do for his Pujan. However, Vishwarup touched his feet and requested to cook again for his Shalagram and take Prasad then.

At last, he was convinced and little Gour kept under lock and key in a separate room. Soon little Gour slept inside the room. After preparation of food, the ascetic started to offer food to God. At the same time somehow all slept but Lord Gouranga awoke and reached the place. He said to the ascetic, "What I should do when you meditate me after cooking? See it is I whom you like to worship."

Chaturbhuj Bal Krishna

The devotee was astonished to find Chaturbhuja Bal Krishna is eating butter with two hands and in other two hands He his about to play the eternal flute.

The ascetic finds Lord Sri Krishna at his front with Sankha, Chakra, Gada, and Lotus in His four hands and also at the next moment he finds Him eating butter in His two hands and other hands are engaged to play the eternal flute. He sees the appearance of Him with precious ornaments on His body; on head peacock's feather and the eternal beauty on the face with nicely garlands on the neck. He also sees the Kadamba tree and Vrindavan with Gopi and cows around Him. Then he looks at the feet decorated with anklets. The guest Brahmin mendicant became senseless. Blessed with the touch of child Gouranga he regained senses but at that time Gouranga disappeared and took bed to continue sleeping as He was sleeping. Except Himself and the mendicant Brahmin, no other could know the incidence.

Elder Vishwarup

Elder brother Vishwarup became a learned boy in his beginning of teens. Often he used to meet older Adwyaitacharya in order to discuss the Gita, the Upanishads etc. Sometime days would almost to pass and the mother Sachidevi used to send little Nemai even in bare body to call Vishwarup. Their houses at Nabadwip were closer. Adwyaitacharya got chances to look at Gouranga.

At last, before the parents were doing arrangements to get Vishwarup married at his sixteen but Vishwarup left home forever in search of God.

Gouranga's Childhood Continues

The parents got pain and sorrow on leaving home by Vishwarup wanted not to give proper education to Gour lest He also becomes ascetic mendicant. He did not take this attempt of parents as granted, as they were impelled with affection and afraid of losing the only son remaining for them. In order to record his protest against this blind affection once Gouranga sat on the heap of dustbin. All neighbours including the parents assembled there and after requests and flattering at last assured Him to send the Chatushpathi - the education center, only then Gour came to them. His learning after the wearing of sacred thread started from the eminent scholar Gangadas. From then Gour would not leave books for a single moment. Shortly Gouranga was a learned personality and people of Nabadwip called Him as 'Nemai Pundit'. However, he had some friends most favourite like Gadadhar, Mukunda, Sanjay, Sriman, Sadashiva and others. With them all Nemai liked to swim in the water of the Ganges and to play with dices.

Other Devotees in Nabadwip

People who used to worship Lord Sri Krishna with the influence of Madhabendra Puri and others all apprehended that Nemai is born to spread the name of

God. His attractive and beautiful personality with sufficient wisdom in Scriptures would always attract all the Sri Krishna worshippers in Nabadwip. They used to listen His splendid narrations sitting aside at the ghat of the river Ganga where Nemai Pundit sat for teaching His students and also to discuss with closed friends. They themselves used to think, if this boy had any love for Lord Sri Krishna, the pain of Sri Krishna followers could be lessened. They prayed for Gourangadev, 'May God bless Him for the love for God'. Sri Baas was one of the elders who astonishingly observed Nemai Pundit.

Father Jagannath

Father Jagannath Mishra arranged the sacred thread of his son Gouranga at his nine. Afterwards, within a short period at the age about sixty he breathed his last.

At the time of his demise son Nemai as a common ordinary boy got shock. He was grieved as if Sri Ramchandra of the Ramayana grieved knowing Raja Dasharatha's death and asked father like a mere child - Who would see me father in your absence?

Jagannath Mishra could utter a few words only - "Sri Ramchandra will look after you. Do not cry. Don't mourn my son."

Lakshmipriya Devi

Some days later, His marriage took place with Lakshmipriya Devi daughter of Ballav Acharya a pious and scholar personality of Nabadwip. This, perhaps, was according to Nemai's own preference and arrangement by Mother Sachidevi.

Sri Gadadhar the Lifelong Partner

On the new moon day of Baisakh in 1408 Saka (in 1487 A.D.) Sri Gadadhar Pundit was born after one and half month (some says one year and one and half months, some say after six years) of Gourangdev's birth. Gadadhar's parents were Madhab Mishra and Ratnadevi. Madhab Mishra came to Nabadwip from Chattragram (Chittagong) of East Bengal and settled at the holy place with scopes of learning and offering education. They were very pious couple, and they were disciples of Madhabendrapuri, the then the most renowned preacher and pioneer of the name of Lord Sri Krishna's Divine love. Some of devotees, till, worship Gadadhar as Radharani the main strength of Lord Sri Krishna.

Sri Gadadhar was the constant companion of Mahaprabhu from the time of their childhood. However, we surprisingly noticed that only a few writers during the five centuries have written the glory of Gadadhar Pundit. Some have also averted the topic on Gadadhar. Gadadhar-Gouranga lived in closer houses in the same locality. Gadadhar's mother Ratnavati Devi often used to meet Sachidevi. Sachidevi took her as own sister. Gouranga and Gadadhar used to play together on the yard nearer to where their mothers generally used to sit and talk each other sometimes at Mahaprabhu's house and sometimes at Gadadhar's house. They both studied together at the same school. Nemai could not remain without Gadadhar even for a moment and Gadadhar likewise couldn't stand to be separated from Nemai. Naturally, younger Gadadhar got much affection from Nemai.

From very childhood, Gadadhar was an honest, humble, soft, with loveable character and used to worship and serve for Lord Sri Krishna. He remained with Sri Chaitanyadev until the last moment of Lila on this earth. All the Vaishnavas of all the sections believe that Lord Narayana, Lord Ramchandra, Lord Basudeva, Lord Sri Krishna, appeared himself as Gouranga Mahaprabhu in the Koliyuga and Gadadhar remained as the power of God all the ages. Therefore, devotees believe Gadadhar as Brishabhanu's daughter Vrindavaneswari Radharani and most beloved of Lord Sri Krishna of His eternal Vrindavan Lila. Gadadhar was likewise regarded by a few devotees. During the Nabadwip Lila Gadadhar used to decorate Mahaprabhu.

""Srila Swarupa Damodara has written in his diary—

Avani sura bavah Sri Panditakhyo jatindrah
Sa khalo bhavati Radha Srila Gauravataro.

Lord Gouranga is beyond the perview of the scriptures, beyond the entire Brahman, and above even the Vedas. Lord Nityananda is His eternal self as Balaram. Lord

Chaitanya is Lord Govinda Himself and Pundita Gadadhar is none other than Sri Radha.

The eminent singer of the time Vasudeva Ghose sang of the beauty of this divine couple - Sri Gaura-Gadadhara -Yugal Deity (combined of the two) (as confirmed in Samsad Bangalee Charitavidhan too) in whose worship he has been completely subjugated. He prays that he will desire to serve them births after births.

In Sri Chaitanya-Charitamrita we likewise find :

"Panditer bhav mudre kahan naa jai,
Gadadhar pran nath nam hoila jay,
Panditer kripa prasad lehan na jay,
Gadai Gauranga kari sarvalokey gaay".

The emotions and expressions of Pundit Gadadhar are not possible to describe. Another name of Lord Gauranga is the 'Lord of the life of Gadadhara.' Who can understand what mercy has been bestowed upon him? Their glories are sung by devotees as "Gadai- Gauranga."

We also can sing-

Jai Goura Gadadhara, Jai Nityananda,
Jai Adwyaita Sri Baasa Gurubhaktavrinda."

3

NEMAI'S VIDYAVILAS

At the age of sixteen after completing necessary education and some days later after father Jagannath Mishra's demise Nemai started a Tole, a school offering education of Sanskrit, specially its Grammar at the open space of yearly worshipping place of the Chandi (called Chandi Mandap), the goddess of power and strength. The place was at Mukunda-Sanjay's house. This time many scholars used to come to Nemai Pundit to discuss several topics. Gadadhar used to be with Gour and Mukunda used to sing nice devotional songs in their meetings.

During the Vidyavilas time, Nemai used to catch friends and even other elderly persons who used to worship Lord Sri Krishna and ask harder questions. Among them the most beloved Gadadhar, Mukunda Murari, others, and even elderly Sri Baas were not spared. Gourangadev also used to advise them to find books and scriptures at home and thereafter to meet. Thus, the future devotees and the companions of Harinam movements were being prepared themselves with proper and deep knowledge and faith in God. Naturally, being defeated to

Gouranga they tried to leave the place as soon as possible and to flee to their homes to find more and more study materials in order to equip themselves with knowledge and wisdom. Thus, the fellows were being prepared with sufficient feed back of knowledge for preaching others who did not feel for devotion for Sri Krishna.

However, Gourangadev did not disclose the secrets of making future associates ready for the long journey ahead.

Raghunath Siromani

We know the episode, that Nemai dropped critical appreciation of Nayashastra (Logic) into the water of the Ganga. The story was like this, One day Nemai and Raghunath Siromani were sailing on the Ganga and were deeply involved in philosophical discussion. Raghunath Siromani had written an anlysis on Nayashastra. Nemai on His friend's request read out own manuscript of Nayashastra. It was so eloquent that His friend became mesmerised but slight unhappy. Raghunath started to weep. Humbly he pronounced that if the writeup of Nemai is published then nobody would read his analysis which was also written on the same topic. After knowing this, sporty Nemai tore His Tika and threw it into the river saying, "Now, you need not be anxious for your writeup any longer. Do not cry for fame, cry for God only,"

Perhaps Mahaprabhu had written more. Mahaprabhu's other writings except the Siksha Slokastaka and a few Slokas are not available.

Ishwarpuri

In the days of Vidyavilas of Nemai Pundit discovered Ishwarpuri. Ishwarpuri, a disciple of Madhabendrapuri, came in Nabdwip in disguise. People could not easily recognize him. However, Nemai on the way of returning home from the Ganga found him and easily understood that the person must be one devotee of Lord Sri Krishna. The person in the most ordinary dress, hiding himself from the eyes of the people of the ruler's intelligence and enemies. At that time, only a few worshippers of Lord Sri Krishna were engaged in preaching the name of God by traveling throughout India. However, he failed to throw dust in the eyes of Nemai. Both recognized one another. They started to discuss on Lord Sri Krishna at house of Gopinath Acharya in Nabadwip where Ishwarpuri got a shelter.

Afterwards Ishwarpuri reached the house where Adwyaitacharya was engaged in worshipping Lord Sri Krishna with Tulsi and water of the Ganga for God's reappearance. Adwyaitacharya even at his first sight could not guess the identity of the new comer. There were present younger Gadadhar and Mukunda also. They also tried of guessing the identity of the new comer and at last, Mukunda started to sing with his God-gifted melodious voice. The song carried great and deep devotion.

On hearing the sweet melodious song full of devotional themes Ishwarpuri lost his senses. Adwyaitacharya understood that a real devotee has reached his house and he embraced the new comer and received him with due respect. Both of them are disciples of Madhabendrapuri. At the temporary residence at Gopinath Acharya's house many people started to assemble to discuss the topics on Lord Sri Krishna with Ishwarpuri. Among them Nemai, Gadadhar, Mukunda were almost regular. Ishwarpuri recognized not only Nemai but also Gadadhar at his first sight. A beautiful boy with polite nature and having faith and love for Lord Sri Krishna, Gadadhar got much affection from Ishwarpuri. He used to read his Krishnalilamritam to Gadadhar everyday.

Digbijayee Pundit Keshaw Kashmiri

Once, one self-styled world-conqueror who defeated hundreds of scholars in Sanskrit in the Country reached in Nabadwip. The conqueror Keshab Kashmiri started to take information of the scholars of Nabadwip and among the probable contesters, he saw the name of Nemai Pundit. One fine afternoon, while wandering in Nabadwip town and different ghats on the bank of the holy Ganga he found Nemai. Nemai Pundit was discussing with some students and scholar listeners. He found Nemai a mere boy of teenaged teaching all with His melodious voice and scholarly expertness. Keshab's companions informed him that it is he whose name topped the list of scholars of Nabadwip.

He introduced himself as world conqueror and Nemai

Pundit showed due respect to him and asked him to describe the glory of the Ganga.

Keshab Kashmiri, then and by composing a poem on the ghat of the holy river started to recite it. In the recitation there were one hundred slokas with which he prayed the Ganga in the poem.

Mahattang Gangayah satatamidabhati nitarang
Yadesha Sri Vishoscharankamalotpatti subhaga.
Ditwiya Sri Lakshmiriba suranarairchaycharana
Bhabanibharturya siroshi bibhatyadbhutaguna.

Nemai found five faults of grammar and rhetoric in the poem. As for example, Bhabani itself is the wife of Bhaba (Lord Shiva) and then husband of Bhabani becomes meaningless.

At last, the conqueror scholar Keshab Kashmiri being defeated to a teen age boy—like Nemi Pundit asked how it was possible for him to recollect a few lines from one hundred slokas and detect five faults.

Humbly Nemai Pundit consoled him and advised to give up vanity forever and to take shelter of Lord Sri Krishna. This is the first time Nemai told one to get shelter in Lord Sri Krishna.

Nemai in East Bengal

Afterwards Gourangadev went to East Bengal to offer education and to arrange future programme. We learnt that Nemai travelled to Dacca, Faridpur districts on the bank of the Padma and Srihatta the district from where father Jagannath Mishra and other scholars immigrated to Nabadwip. He traveled Vikrampore, Subarna village, Egarsindur, Betal etc. and established schools for offering education. Students from different corners started to come to the education centers. There met Tapan Mishra and requested not to leave them. Gourangadev advised him to settle at Varanasi and meet again in future. However, in the mean time Lakshmipriya devi expired suddenly by snakebite in Nabadwip. Probably, feeling the mishap Gourangadev returned to the mother Sachidevi and without asking to anybody understood the reality.

On Return to Nabadwip

Nemai returned home but could not find wife Lakshmipriya there and understood that she has left this earth. Nemai could sense this accident and so returned from East Bengal hurriedly. Nemai then engaged Himself in more learning, teaching and discussions throughout the whole days with other scholars in Nabadwip. Students from different corners of the Country assembled in Nabadwip to receive teachings from famous Nemai Pundit. They learned not only to learn properly but they learned to maintain their own rites for own religion and complete faith in God and complete surrender to Lord Sri Krishna.

Second Marriage with Vishnupriyadevi

The Mother Sachidevi again arranged the marriage of her son Gouranga with a beautiful daughter of Sanatan Mishra Vishnupriya Devi. Buddhimanta Khan (Zeminder Subuddhi Roy) took the entire responsibility of expenditure of the marriage. Buddhimanta Khan was fond of Gourangadev and later he became a pious devotee and settled in Vrindavan with direction from Gourangadev. The marriage became a memorable event in Nabadwip like a marriage of a prince.

In Nabadwip Gourangadev continued teachings at the centre and got immense fame for His scholarly teaching capacity. Students from various corner of the Country used to come to Nabadwip.

Nemai's Visit of Sri Padapadma at Gaya and Initiation

Taking permission from the mother Sachidevi after almost two years after the marriage Nemai Pundit with some followers and maternal uncle Chandra Sekhar went to Gaya for giving Pinda to the deceased father and fore fathers.

After performing the rituals in practice Gourangadev visited the sign of holy Feet of Vishnu and became almost mad for God Vishnu, Lord Sri Krishna. There came, by chance, Ishwarpuri who once met Gouranga before in Nabadwip. Gourangadev observing his devotion in Lord

Sri Krishna became overwhelmed and wanted to get initiation and thus Ishwarpuri by giving the Sri Krishna Mantra became the preceptor of Sri Gourangadev. He got the mantra of Lord Sri Krishna. After visiting the birth place of Ishwarpuri at Kumarhatta Sri Gourangadev came back to mother Sachidevi in Nabadwip but a changed person who always thinks of God Lord Sri Krishna.

4

NABADWIP LILA COMMENCES

From then Gourangadev appeared to be a new personality and started to see God Sri Krishna everywhere and started to sing, dance, cry for Lord Sri Krishna. He did not remain as Nemai Pundit, neither as Bishwambhar, nor Gouranga only but became Mahaprabhu Sri Gouranga who was mad for Lord Sri Krishna. On the other side the people few in number who wished that Nemai Pundit should have faith in Sri Krishna instead of leaving practices of teasing, embarrassing the Krishna loving people in times, were surprised to note the modesty and the attraction to Sri Krishna, love for Sri Krishna, thirst for the darshan of 'entwined in bliss Krishna and Radha'.

Thirst and Quest for Lord Sri Krishna

One morning some followers of Sri Krishna were plucking flowers and Tulsi leaves at a flower garden for worshipping Sri Krishna at their own houses. There were Gadadhar, Gopinath, Ramai, Sribaas and some others. Sriman Pundit hurriedly came to them and announced that Gouranga has become modest one. He does not show any audacity to anybody. He becomes mad whenever listens the name of Lord Sri Krishna by any body. Gouranga shall express the experiences of Gaya tour.

Sriman Pundit added any body could meet the meeting at Shuklambar's residence in the afternoon. In the afternoon at Shuklambar Brahmachari's residence Gadadhar took shelter by hiding himself for hearing what Gouranga would say. Gouranga came to the house with tilting body, as the heart is always full of Sri Krishna.

He cries — "Where is Krishna. Krishna was seen here, now where He has gone." Other Krishna followers also feeling Lord Krishna's presence and some were weeping in love for God. Gouranga advised Murari and Sadashiva to worship Lord Krishna with more respect.

Gadadhara, however, could not restrain his ecstasy. With his head bowed down, he continued to cry very loudly.

Hearing his pitiful sobbing, Gouranga Mahaprabhu enquired—

Who is there weeping?

Murari answered - It is Gadadhar. Yours Gadadhar.'

With the words 'yours Gadadhar' one can easily understand how Gadadhar was closet to Gourangadev.

Sri Gourangadev called Gadadhar with much affection and Gadadhar leaving the hiding corner of the room of Suklambar Brahmachari came out and fell on the feet of Gourangadev. He told Gadadhar—

'Your life is successful as you are worshipping Lord Sri Krishna from the childhood. Alas, I have lost the time without worshipping Krishna.' By saying this, Mahaprabhu Sri Gouranga embraced Gadadhar in great love and again fainted.

Sri Gouranga Mahaprabhu, upon coming from Gaya Dham, day and night He floated in the ocean of love of Sri Krishna. Gadadhara, upon seeing the Gouranga Mahaprabhu showering of tears in love for Sri Krishna, also began to cry in ecstatic love.

Gadadhar Pundit always remains at Mahaprabhu's side

One day Sri Gadadhara brought some pan (betal leaf) to Sri Gauranga, who, in an exuberance of emotion asked him—

"Gadadhara! Where is that beautiful Blackish Boy who is dressed in yellow garments?" After asking this, Gouranga Mahaprabhu began to shed tears.

Gadadhar respectfully suggested—

"He is in your heart."

Hearing this, Mahaprabhu began to tear his chest with his nails, but Gadadhar quickly grabbed his hands. Mahprabhu said to him, "Gadadhara! Leave me. I cannot remain a moment more not seeing Sri Krishna."

Gadadhar replied, "Just try to be a little patient and please calm Yourself. Krishna will come any moment here and everywhere."

Hearing this, Mahaprabhu became somewhat composed.

Sachimaa heard all these and then seeing Gadadhara's ability to control her Nemai became very pleased with Gadadhar. She declared, "Though He is just a boy, He is very intelligent. I am frightened to go before my son when He is in these moods. But Gadadhar has very cleverly pacified him."

Sachimaa told Gadadhar—"Gadadhara! You must please remain with Nemai always. If you stay with Him then I won't have to worry."

Since then, on Nemai's Sannyas He remained at Puri in order to serve his beloved Nemai. Gadadhar Pundit kept the words of a mother till the last moment on this earth.

Increased Love for Sri Krishna

A few days passed but day after day Sri Gouranga's love for Sri Krishna increased. He forgot to go to Tole to teach the students. Condition of the family and social reality were neglected. The once teacher Gangadas Pundit came and suggested Gouranga to pay attention to the students came from far, otherwise how the family would be maintained? Gouranga nodded the head and with the students started coaching. One day with the students roaming in the town reached the door of Ratnagarva Pundit. Nemai Pundit was discussing with them. After a few hours Ratnagarva was returning home by reciting one pair of lines from the Srimadbhagabata. On hearing the recitation Gourangadev fainted in love of Lord Sri Krishna. It is obvious that Gadadhar remains where Gouranga remains or moves. Seeing fainted Gadadhar somehow nursed with the help of the students and requested Ratnagarva to stop. Gouranga getting sense again requested Ratnagarva to recite the very lines.

The Picture of the Sloka cited by Ratnagarva

> *"Shyamang hiranyaparidhing banamalyabahrdhatu prabal nataveshamnubratangse,*
> *Binyastahastamitayena yunanabjam karnotpalala kapolmukhabjalasan."*

The very lines (10/ 23/22) were of a picture on the incidence of Sri Krishna darshan by the wives of Yagnik i.e. burnt offering Brahmins. Their villages were nearer to grazing grounds where young Krishna with elder brother Balaram and other children from the houses of milkmen use to allow their cows and calves for gazing. Coming to the grounds perhaps they have eaten up the tiffin supplied by their mothers. In the noon, they felt hungry and young Krishna guessed sure the Brahmin ladies have prepared food for their husbands, children and other members of their families. Krishna's team of hungry children at first went to them but the ladies rejected their requests of surrendering food. On this refusal, Krishna advised them to struggle until they achieve the prayed things - Go and ask for. Go again and again once you would succeed'. He also advised them to inform the ladies of the Brahmins that son Gopal of Nandagopa, God Himself has favoured them by asking for food.

Realizing the eternal truth the women came to Krishna with the entire food they prepared for their husbands and children. They saw all the Gopa children, Sri Krishna and Sri Balaram on the bank of the Yamuna River.

The description in the recitation of Ratnagarva was- "His complexion is beautiful dark blue. He is wearing a yellow coloured dress. There is garland with the flowers from nearby forests around His neck. He is decorated as an actor of a certain drama with peacock's feather, metals like gold, coral sand others. He has placed one of his hands on shoulder of one companion and circling another hand the lotus of the eternal creativity. Earrings under the ears, hair clinging from the head are disarranged and the eternal laughter remaining on the lips of Sri Krishna".

Gadadhar somehow managed to take Gouranga at home where Sachimaa is waiting for her son eagerly.

Samkirtan in Nabadwip

Gourangadev started the movement of introduction and circulation of Harinaam. At first started at Chandrasekhar's house and at own home then continuously at the house of Sri Baas. Gouranga roams here and there in Nabdwip at the ghats of the Ganges and tries to establish scriptures and theories with students and scholars. One day Gour enters the cluster of houses of the weavers. All gather around Gouranga and after giving due repects all gifted their products. Although Gouranga offered the actual price of each product they denied taking any price. Then Gouranga enters the cluster of houses of milkmen and they bring curd, milk, butter etc. for Mahaprabhu and offer without taking price. Then

Mahaprabhu comes to houses of businessmen of cosmetics and scents and they with due respect gifted Gouranga their products for use. Gouranga reached the houses of flower and garland sellers and they decorated the Godly body of Mahaprabhu with sufficient flowers and garlands. Gouranga met the petal (Pan) seller and he took Mahaprabhu as his fortune and with regards offered pan for chewing. The conch seller also presented a Godly conch. Thus, Gouranga Mahaprabhu roamed thousands of houses of ordinary people of different traders and businessmen and interacted irrespective of rich and poor. All considered His presence as their fortune.

Chaturbhuja and Dwibhuja

Then Gouranga reached the house of Sarbgna. Sarbagna by, remembering Gopal sees Gouranga Mahaprabhu as four handed holding the Sankha, the Chakra, the Gada, and the Padma (conch, circle, club and lotus). He sees again two handed with butter in hands and the flute tied at the waist. He also sees Lord Sri Krishna in a mood of bending three parts of His body.

Sridhar and Other Common Men

Afterwards Gourangadev reaches the hut of Sridhar. Sridhar is one of the poorest traders in market. He used to sell cone and skin of banana tree cheaper things and somehow he maintained his livelihood. Mahaprabhu used to make fun with him almost everyday in the market or on his returning hut with unsold materials. Mahaprabhu liked cone and skin of banana tree and sometime snatched from him saying that he is much rich.

Here at his hut Gouranga Mahaprabhu did the same fun by gratifying him. He felt himself the most fortunate, as he was a true devotee of Lord Sri Krishna. He offered leaves, skin and cone of banana to Nemai Pundit. He also gifted one of his bottle-guard from the wretched thatched roof of his hut. Having made some fun with Sridhar Gouranga returned home.

Sachidevi then listens the Godly flute playing her son only. In this way Gouranga Mahaprabhu favoured all the common people, small ordinary and well to do traders and the rich of Nabadwip.

5

GADADHAR REMAINS WITH GOURANGADEV

Gourangadev could see the whole scene whenever the words of the recitation by Ratnagarva enter into the ears. Being deeply thoughtful of Lord Sri Krishna Gouranga Mahaprabhu cannot resist Himself from fainting. Getting senses Gourangadev could see Sri Krishna in the front as if He can be touched. All devotees like to see Him throughout their lives but Sri Gouranga got the chances to see to touch God the Lord Sri Krishna all the time so Gourangadev fainted often. Even in the presence of mother Sachidevi. She cannot manage her son herself but Gadadhar could manage his friend within a moment. Once he told Gourangadev that God remains in Him and He tries to tear His chest Gadadhar protects saying, - You know better that God remains in everybody's heart but it is not that to see Him by tearing heart, it is only to feel Him in you. By seeing Gadadhar's ability to control Gouranga mother Sachidevi requested Gadadhar to be always with Gouranga. Gadadhar kept the words until the last moment in the earth in Neelachal. Thus Gadadhar remained the most beloved and constant companion of Gourangadev.

Harinaam Movement

Now Gourangadev started the 'Harinaam movement at the house of Sri Baas. There joined Gadadhar, Sanjay, Mukunda, Chandrasekhar, Suklambar Brahmachari an ordinary beggar but a devotee of Lord Sri Krishna and also Sridhar an ordinary cone seller but silently a devotee of Lord Sri Krishna and more other followers. The earlier devotees of Lord Sri Krishna all who used to repent that Nemai Pundit having such beautiful qualities and unbelievable wisdom and knowledge always prefer to disturb Krishna-devotees instead of worshipping Sri Krishna has now become fully changed, joined the Samkirtan. These people who were afraid of now do not avoid Gourangadev rather they enthusiastically became part and parcel of Harinaam Samkirtan. Day after day the number of participants increased. Now Sri Gouranga is more soft and modest. His behaviour to all is so sweet that all became His followers.

Adwyaitacharya Has Been Informed of

Some of the devotees rushed to Adwyaitacharya. They informed him that Vidyavilas days' Nemai Pundit is a changed one and started Harinaam Samkirtan at Sribaas's house every night. Nemai Pundit i.e. Gourngadev is engaged in Harinaam all the hours. Adwyaitacharya earlier known as Kamalaksha

Bhattacharya who desired that liberator from all evils in the society will soon reappear has become delighted. He told the persons who brought the information that his dream of Lord's appearance is getting success. He also assured them that in proper time he would join Him. He expected that in need Gourangadev would call him and he would be remainig for His call.

Was Mahaprabhu mad ?

On the other hand people who could not feel the situation started to announce that Gouranga has become almost mad and needs proper treatment. Sachimaa naturally became worried for her only son. So one day she came to Sribaas and asked whether it is true that Nemai's craziness has reached in so acute position that an early treatment is required? Sribaas replied that they everybody would be happy if the same disease occupies them. Nemai is the leader of Harinaam and is now quite well. Somehow, Sribaas consoled her.

Along with Sri Gadadhar, Gourangadev met Adwyaitacharya

Adwyaitacharya has been informed of but one day Mahaprabhu decided to meet him because the elder person wanted to see that someone would appear to save the creations. So, Mahaprabhu with lifetime partner Gadadhar met Adwyaitacharya. Now Adwyaitacharya becomes pleased to see the grown up Gourangadev at his front. To see Him Adwyaitacharya started to worship with

Pujan materials so that the society and the Country would get rid of all types of mischiefs, misconduct. Gadadhar stares at both of them with surprise and believes that now God has really reappeared.

"Ekdin Prabhu Gadadhare kori sangey
Adwait dekhitey Prabhu chalilen rangey"

Haridas the Most Beloved Devotee

We have learnt that from his childhood Haridas joined Sri Adwyaitacharya. Haridas was born in 1371 Saka in a village Buran in the district Nadia. His father Sumati thakur brethed his last when he was only a six years' old. Then his mother Gouridevi had also courted death by burning herself on her husband's funeral pyre. Haridas at his six became parentless and a pious Muslim family brought him up as their own son. Having shelter like a son in a Muslim family as usual he read the Qur'an. Haridas afterwards being aware of God's oneness and glory met Sri Adwyaitacharya at Shantipur and requested to give him Krishna Mantra. After repeated requests and having observed some signs of Bhakti Adwyaitacharya gave him the Mantra-

Hare Krishna Hare Krishna Krishna Krishna Hare Hare
Hare Rama Hare Rama Rama Rama Hare Hare.

With this Mantra modest Haridas settled in a hut in the village Kulia and started to take the mantra on rosary almost all the time.

He was known as Yaban Haridas.Once a local Kazi ordered him not to utter Hare Krishna as Hindus. He denied to obey the orders so, he was beaten in twentytwo market places but did not leave the name of Lord Sri Krishna and somehow he survived with uttering Hare Krishna mantra.

Gourangadev with Associates at Sri Baas Angan

The house of Sri Baas now became full of grandeur with this new inclusion. Still Mahaprabhu awaited Adwyaitacharya. He came to Nabadwip from Shantipur but did not meet the team. His presence in Nabadwip was felt by Sri Gouranga and sent Ramai Pundit to bring him. With his wife Adwyaitacharya reached there and joined the team of Samkirtan. The whole Nabadwip was full of the name of Lord Sri Krishna. Now Sri Gouranga has a team where an older and experienced devotee Adwyaitacharya, polite and deep devotee of Lord Sri Krishna and above all lifetime companion Gadadhar, a man dedicated life only in Harinaam Haridas, Basudev Dutta and his brother having a sweet voice singer and devotee Mukunda, a devotee of Ramchandraji Murai, others like Chandrasekhar, Sadashiv, Sanjay, Sridhar, Suklambar Brahmachari all other devotees are present in the house of Sri Baas with his brothers.

6

NITYANANDAPRABHU JOINS THE TEAM

Gouranga Mahaprabhu with the associates at Sri Baas angan remain fully engaged in Samkirtan day and night. It started at the house of Suklambar Brahmachari. For someday it continued at Mahaprabhu's house but lastly Sri Baas himself offered his house for this Samkirtan. One night Mahaprabhu got signs in a dream that somebody is coming. He found in dream that a great Abadhut with a large figure wearing a dress in blue colour stepped from a chariot.

On the other hand, Nityananda felt that Sri Gouranga Mahaprabhu has started Samkirtan in Nabadwip and he from Vrindavan reached Nabadwip.

Nityananda was born on Tuesday, the 12th/(13th) of January in 1474 (1395 Saka, in the month of Magha Sukla Traodashi in Bengali Sal 880) in the village of Ekchakra in the district of Birbhum. His father Harai Pundit known as Haru Ojha (some say Mukunda) and mother Srimati Padmadevi were also a pious couple. They had seven sons, they were Nityananda, Krishnanda, Brahmananda, Purnananda, Premananda and Vishuddhananda. Parents used to call Nityananda in the name Kuber.

From his childhood he was fond of playing with friends near a Shiva Temple. His playing almost was of acting dramas from the stories of the Ramayana and the Bhagawat etc. Puranas with all mates. One day at the time of acting as Lakshman in Indrajit Badh drama made spontaniously by themselves Nityananda fainted. All the villagers including Padmadevi and Harai Pundit rushed to their playground and tried to bring his senses but could not. At last one of the children co-actors as the Hanuman ran into a jungle and brought some bush from which some petals rubbed on Kuber he woke up.

At the age of only twelve reached a mendicant Vaishnav in their house and for his service elder son Nityananda was appointed. The mendicant was very pleased with the family and with the services rendered by Nityananda. At the time of leaving the house of Harai Ojha he begged Nityananda for his assistance during his roaming throughout the vast land. At that time the people could not decline any pious medicant vaishnav. However, the parents at last with lot of aches agreed to leave their elder son Nityananda with him.

The madicant with Nityananda reached upto Bakreswar in the Birbhum district. Alone from Bakreswar he started to travel through Baidyanath, Gaya, Varanasi on foot. The information about the medicant is not available. Nityananda was alone. Therefore, Nityananda had to receive lot of obstacles, confronted with different situations and came across varied experiences. In this twenty years some time he had to live on fasting or only water or milk or with whatever food. Sometime he had to take rest or sleep under any tree in forest or in cave or at any bank of a river. From twelve to thirtytwo during these twenty years Nityananda roamed alone sometime with some unknown teams of Sannyasis all over the Country.

Once in the western India, accidentally he found the pioneer Madhabendra Puri with his disciples like Iswarpuri and others. Some guess that Nityananda as spent a long time with them he got initiation from Madhabendra Puri. Some also guess that Nityananda here knew the news of Upserge of Mahaprabhu Sri Gouranga.

Nityananda came to Nabadwip and took shelter at Nandan Acharya's house. On the other hand, Mahaprabhu was searching for him but his associates Sri Bas and Haridas could not find. At last, Mahaprabhu Gourangadev with all associates Himself reached the house of Nandan Acharya and found Nityananda as Abadhut Sannyasi like dress but with blue colour. Nityananda seated erect at the portico of the house. Both of them looked at each other. For a few moments, none could speak a single word. The stout body tall and sun-tanned fair complexion with tears in eyes for Lord Sri Krishna made Gourangadev confident that this person's shoulder would be the right choice of spreading the name of Sri Krishna among all the people irrespective of castes and colors.

Sri Baas and Vrindavandas

Vrindavan Das had written the one of the most authentic and important Life Sketch of Gourangadev 'Sri Chaitanya Bhagabata'. Completed the writing within fifteen years of divine disappearance of Mahaprabhu.

Sri Baas's father Jaladhar Pundit had five sons. They were Nalini, Sri Baas, Sri Ram (Ramai Pundit), Sripati and Srinidhi. Elder Nalini expired and so his daughter Narayani was brought up with fatherly affection by Sri Baas.

Narayani was blessed by Gouranga Mahaprabhu with His eaten rest foodstuff when she was only four years' old. She was married to a Brahmin bridegroom named Baikunthanath. But before or just after the birth of son Baikunthanath suddenly expired. So considering the awkward position of Narayani as she became fatherless and husbandless but carrying a child, Sri Baas took her back at his house at Kumarhatta. Vrindavan Das was born in Krishna Dwadashi of Baisakh 1429 Saka there (as referred by HKM is GBS from Prem Vilas).

Six handed Sri Krishna

One day Mahaprabhu advised Nityananda to worship Vyas. He gave a garland to Nityananda and Nityananda saw Gouranga Mahaprabhu. He found that Mahaprabhu is Himself six handed Sri Krishna with conch, wheel arms, club, lotus, a plough, and a mallet in his six hands. Nityananda fainted to see this.

Gourangadev strictly advised all not to disregard other gods and goddesses; to give equal respect to Lord Krishna, Shiva and Ram also.

Gadadhar with Mukunda met Pundarik Vidyanidhi

One day an excellent singer and a closed company Mukunda came to Gadadhar and said to him if he wants to see an actual Vaishnav (who worships Sri Krishna seriously) he may go with him. There he may see a Vaishnav who has come from district of Chittagong of East Bengal.

At the first sight, any body would tell the person enjoys earthly materials and consumes rich food.

At first sight, Gadadhar also thought himself at what place and at what person Mukunda has brought him. However, with Mukunda Gadadhar bowed at his feet as usual like Mukunda. Mukunda introduced Gadadhar with Pundarik Vidyanidhi. Pundarik Vidyanidhi was a disciple of Madhabendrapuri, like Sri Adyaitacharya, Ishwarpuri, Madhab Mishra and Nityananda. However, Pundarik Vidyanidhi was well dressed with valuable clothes. Having seated on a luxurious seat, at both of his sides two persons were fanning him with beautiful hand fans. The roof of the place was full of decoration for his stay. With the rich fragrances, it appeared perhaps he has used valuable cosmetics and fragrant materials. He was taking Pan with scented ingredients. Gadadhar could not feel satisfied at the first sight. All these made Gadadhar laugh. To see the luxurious style he leads for himself Gadadhar felt embarrassed and he wanted to say his company Mukunda to leave the place. Until the day, Gadadhar has seen almost all Vaishnavas are like most ordinary men or poor or beggar. Gadadhar is fond of Gouranga Mahaprabhu and he has seen him from the childhood. He has seen his father Madhab Mishra, Adwyaitacharya, Ishwarpuri, Sri Baas and some other vaishnavas in simple manner. In addition, he wanted to see an actual Vaishnab not a princelike behave.

Mukunda perhaps could read the mind of his friend Gadadhar. Mukunda started to sing a song on Putana. Once King Kansa wanted to kill newborn child Krishna and he tried much but failed. Among many efforts one of his efforts was sending Putana Rakshas to Nandalaya where child Krishna was lying. In disguise Putana reached the house of Nanda and took the child in her lap like a neighbouring lady and hidingly she poured her breast covered with strong poison into the mouth of child Krishna and Krishna as an ordinary child gave a bite deeply which Putana could not tolerate and died there. Everybody came to know the truth. However, Lord Sri Krishna at the beginning gave her the respect of a mother so He took her breast into His mouth when she was pouring it. Mukunda's song in melodious voice with devotion the glory of lord Sri Krishna made Pundarik Vidyanidhi almost mad. He remembered Sri Krishna. He forgot his dresses, forgot the pot of Pan, he danced on the floor. All luxurious goods were disarranged and destroyed, but he did not care, he danced and sang with Mukunda madly.

It continued for sometime and Gadadhar observing the deep devotion and feeling for Lord Krishna in Pundarik Vidyanidhi thanked his company Mukunda. In addition, Gadadhar informed him that he wants to beg apology to Vidyanidhi because at first sight he thought him otherwise.

Gadadhar's Decision for Initiation and Mahaprabhu's Approval

At last, Gadadhar asked for mantra to him and Vidyanidhi expressed his happiness as he would get a disciple like Gadadhar so polite and gentle and devotee of Lord Sri Krishna from the childhood. Gadadhar asked permission from Gourangadev. He also not only approved but also shown His full satisfaction on the matter that His Gadadhar will get a capable preceptor. Therefore, Gourangadev advised to expedite the matter of his initiation.

Team more Enlarged

All the participants noted earlier that Gourangadev was waiting for someone to come and that became fulfilled with the adoption of Pundarik Vidyanidhi from Chittagong. Both Mahaprabhu and Vidyanidhi embraced each other and drenched with the tears for Lord Sri Krishna. The Samkirtan continued in full swing. The waves of Samkirtan now reached the houses of ordinary citizens of Nabadwip and of the Country.

Disturbances, Jagai and Madhai

Many people could not accept the Harinaam Samkirtan easily. They thought this movement would hamper their habits of consuming meat and liquor and their various means to exploit the poor and illiterate people. The heads of the society who used to live on the incomes of the poor and illiterate masses became furious and their propaganda against Mahaprabhu and His team day after day accumulated. Among them there were two officials born in Brahmin family addicted to liquor all the days and always used to tease and disturb the devotees. Gourangadev came to know and He sent Haridas and Nityananda to impress upon them. They were Jagai and Madhai. At the first attempt Haridas and Nityananda had to flee from them as they drove them out. Mahaprabhu sent them again to convince Jagai and Madhai.

Haridas and Nityananda faced them. They told them:-

"Bolo Krishna Bhajo Krishna Kaho Krishna Naam,
Krishna Mata Krishna Pita Krishna Dhan Pran".

Being highly intoxicated with liquor, Madhai suddenly beat nearer Nityananda and then and there his forehead started to bleed. On hearing the news Gouranga Mahaprabhu rushed the place and to see the bleeding He became furious in anger. He wanted to crash them with the Chakra but Nityananda himself saved them from the hands of Lord Gouranga. Jagai and Madhai both realized their mistakes. Gourangadev told Madhai to apologize to Nityananda. By praying apology they enrolled themselves in the Team of Harinaam movement. In the house of Sri Baas they sang in praise to Gouranga Mahaprabhu seated with Gadadhar at the left and Nityananda at the right side.

Samkirtan Movement got Momentum

Within a few days, the Samkirtan movement got momentum. The news of Gouranga Mahaprabhu's Samkirtan movement spread all the important places like pilgrimage centers all over India. Mahaprabhu led all his associates in social work also. One day He himself participated in cleaning and washing some unhealthy temple yards and the areas. To maintain discipline in the Team He segregated the Team in different parts under one chief and one expert singer. He remained on the apex and with option to join each section with Nityananda at His right and Gadadhar at His left all the time. In the mega Samkirtan when all are engaged in singing and dancing Adwyaitacharya touched the feet of Lord Gouranga hiding and some who could notice became surprised to see the act of a senior person to bow his head to junior in age Gouranga Mahaprabhu.

Gouranga Mahaprabhu Himself is Lord Sri Krishna

But many of devotees now wants to believe that Gouranga Mahaprabhu Himself is Lord Sri Krishna,

Nityananda is Balaram, Krishna's elder brother and Gadadhar is Sri Radha the main source of power. Radha and Krishna are inseparable, they are eternal and the One. The Greatest One, the Brahma, 'Satchidananda parama bigraha' is the Lord Sri Krishna and the only One of the Universe. Therefore, it is natural that, not only Adwyaitacharya but also each creature will like to bow their heads under the feet of the Greatest One. To thousands of devotees Sri Gouranga Mahaprabhu has appeared as Lord Sri Krishna. And they started to believe Him the last Incarnation of the Kaliyug.

7

DRAMA-LAKSHMIKAACHH

Drama is also an apparatus of publicity of thoughts that Mahaprabhu knew well. He planned for a drama. Gourangadev Himself composed a drama plot in mind and that was acted by all His followers. Well to do and having some experience Buddhimanta Khan arranged different costumes etc. Stage was erected in the open space at the housc of Chandrasekhar Acharya.

Haridas the Curtain Raiser

At the first entrance of the first act Haridas dressed in costumes entered as joiner to recite the prologue. He announced himself as the Kotwal the chief of police administration of thc Hcavcn.

Gourangadev as Rukmini

Gadadhar was to act as Rukmini. However, being absorbed in emotion Gouranga Mahaprabhu Himself appeared in the dress of Rukmini. Rukmini is writing a letter to Krishna for His coming to her and to rescue her before Sishupal comes and marry her. Her earnest request to save her from the hands of Sishupal, Mahaprabhu becomes absorbed in the emotion. Rukmini was devoted to Lord Sri Krishna throughout all her lives. She is regarded as Lakshmi in Puranas.

Episode of Rukmini by Michael Madhusudhan Dutta

Here we can remember that the episode of Rukmini also moved a Bengali poet and so got importance in the writing of Michael Madhusudhan Dutta (1824-1873). In his 'Virangana' poems among eleven letters one is a letter from Rukmini daughter of Vidarva king Vishmak to the leader of Dwarka, Krishna with a request to rescue her form the hands of Sishupal who was scheduled to come and marry her.

Gadadhar in the Dress of Rama, Lakshmi, Radharani

In the Second Act, Gadadhar entered on the stage as Rukmini with one companion in the dress of Subhadra. Drama continued in full swing. Thereafter, Gadadhar danced as Roma the wife of Lord Narayan, Sri Krishna. Having nice look Gadadhar with fine make-up with ornaments and richly dressed could easily steal the hearts of the audience. All felt Gadadhar is the Lakshmi the eternal wife of Lord Narayana, Sri Krishna. Vrindavandas in his Sri Chaitanya Bhagabat has written:-

"Preme nadi bahey Gadadharer nayaney
Prithwi hoiya sikta dhanya heno maaney
Gadadhar haila yeno Ganga moortimoti
Satya satya Gadadhar Krishner prakriti."

Here the reality of the Drama and the truth of the belief are mixed as he cited twice the word 'Satya' with a belief that Gadadhar is the 'Hladini' power Radharani of Lord Sri Krishna in the past ages of the eternity.

Vrindavandas knew that without important role and all-time presence of Gadadhar the writing of Life-sketch of Sri Chaitanyadev would hardly be possible. So he wrote:

"Jai Jai Goudsimha Srisachikumara
Jai sarba tapahara charan tomaara
Jai Gadadhar prannath mohasaya
Kripa karo prabhu yeno totey mon roi."

Others in the Drama

Adwyaitacharya appeared on the stage in disguise. Nityananda took part as Barhai. Sri Baas appeared as Narad. Each actor was so expertly dressed as the character of the imaginary drama that no one of the audience although all came from their own houses could easily recognize own men.

Vrindavandas was a disciple of Prabhu Nityananda but he paid equal attention to draw the life sketches of Gadadhar Pundit and others in the Sri Chaitanya Bhagawat.

8

SRI BAAS ANGAN AT THE PEAK

Sri Baas Angan (yard of the house) now became saturated with the Samkirtan led by Gouranga Mahaprabhu. Different teams as segregated by Mahaprabhu participated in the dances and songs of Lord Sri Krishna. Outsiders were not allowed to enter in the house because without proper devotion to Lord Sri Krishna others may make create confusion. In the Samkirtan, sometimes Gouranga Mahaprabhu becomes senseless and the followers also become senseless. He felt, after gaining sense, the Samkirtan has reached the peak and the necessity to spread Samkirtan among all. He advised to perform Samkirtan with musical apparatus like Dhole, Kansi, Conch, etc. as used domestically in the pujas of Durga the mother, Sri Chandi, Bishahari and other gods and goddesses of power and available at everybody's house and in absence of instruments people can use their hands for clapping with the songs for Lord Sri Krishna.

The Satyagraha Movement

It was time of Chanting the name of Sri Krishna on the Streets of Nabadwip.

The news of Samkirtan movement got much circulation and some people who were afraid of reforms complained to the Kazi, the chief of local administration. Having belief in a different religion Kazi at primary level did not interfere in the Samkirtan Movement. However being provoked from some people of Nabadwip naturally Kaji agreed to make some disturbances by smashing musical instruments and ultimately passed orders to ban the Harinaam Movement. On hearing this order Gouranga Mahaprabhu then and there took the decision to protest against such orders opposing personal rights. In organized way, thousands of people and devotees stepped on the main road and made a long protest-rally with songs for Lord Sri Krishna on their lips and burning torches in waiving hands. The rally on its way was enlarging as thousands of citizens spontaneously joined the procession. Some were singing :-

"Haraye Namah Krishna Yadabaya Namah
Gopal Gobinda Rama Sri Madhusudana."

Some sang-*Tuar Charane Mon Laguhure*

Sarangadhara Tuar Charane Mon Laguhure" and some sang other songs on Lord Sri Krishna.

"Vijay hoila Hari Nandaghoser Bala
Hari Hari heathey banshi galey banamala."

At last Mahaprabhu with all reached the village Simalia where Kazi dwells. Kazi went in hiding in fear of the power of the mass. Some uncontrollable participants messed up flower gardens, roofs of the rooms but Mahaprabhu rudely ordered them to stop and He with the help of some gentle company called Kazi from inside the house. Having witnessed the power of the mass and convincing words of Mahaprabhu Kazi ultimately was bound to withdraw the orders of banning Samkirtan. Thus openly singing i.e. 'Kirtan' in Bengal got license from the Ruling Authority.

News of this triumphant movement without any arms but only with songs and dances in the name of Lord Sri Krishna and Lord Gouranga Mahaprabhu reached other places of the Country.

Now it is time to go forward with the name of Lord Sri Krishna. He advised the masses to pray silently or on rosary. He advised all of His followers and the people to chant the name of Lord Sri Krishna with whatever musical instruments they have at hand at home for prayer silently or on rosary : -

"Hare Krishna Hare Krishna Krishna Krishna Hare Hare
Hare Rama Hare Rama Rama Rama Hare Hare".

Worshipping of Sri Vishnu

One day Gourangadev decided to worship Sri Vishnu at the house of Sri Baas. All arrangements were made. Mahaprabhu sat for the puja but His mind was thoroughly engrossed with the love for Sri Vishnu. His dresses were drenched with the tears that fell from His eyes. Getting senses back He left the seat and bathed and wearing another set of fresh dress. Again the incidence of coming tears happened. Again He bathed and wore fresh dress but the same state repeated. At last Gouranga

Mahaprabhu advised His next person Gadadhar to sit on the seat and to worship Sri Vishnu.

People Regained Self Confidence

Now Nabadwip Lila is a matured movement but the name of Lord Sri Krishna should be spread over rest of the vast Country. The' Krishna naam movement has wiped out the caste system and other differences among the ordinary people. People cite Kirtan all along and regained self confidence. They can believe that they are men. This self respect gave them tremendous enthusiasm of being active in all respects. So changes were observed everywhere even in the fields of cultivation and small industry and specially in the fields of literature. Because people were learnt to work in hand and to utter the name of Lord Sri Krishna on lips. They knew to live happily.

Mahaprabhu cannot sit idle at home or with lovely wife and to maintain family only by the profession of teaching at school. He is to do more for Lord Sri Krishna. He is to see other places and contact with people at various places in the Country. He is to do more things for the society. He is to lead all to wipe out caste system from the Country. He is to preach everyone that each man is same, as everyone possesses 'Atman' or 'Jibatma' an atomic particle of God the 'Paramatma'.

9

DECISION OF SANNYAS

Once He decided to go outside home and become an ascetic. His decision was disclosed to only six persons. They were Sachi Devi the mother, Gadadhar the constant company, Brahmananda, Chandrasekhar maternal uncle, Mukunda and Nityananda on whose shoulder the responsibility of all Vaishnavas of Goud-Bengal later were rest upon. All of the six persons tried to make understand that worshipping of Lord Sri Krishna is also possible by remaining at home within own family. However, Lord Gouranga preferred not to say at home for worshipping Lord Sri Krishna for ownself. He is to make others understand that in Kaliyug only Krishna naam is the vow. On understanding this Sachimaa kept herself silent and could not weep as Vishnupriya the wife of Gouranga Mahaprabhu and others having known the news well before may create trouble. Especially Vishnupriya will not be able to bear with such news of Sannyas. (Although she, afterwards, had to admit this separation. She remained at home with a pair of wooden pedal only with her mother-in-law Sachidevi.)

The day came. It was the last day, the Sankranti of Pousha in the year 1431 Saka (16th day of January 1510

A.D.) Someone gave Sachimaa a bottle-gourd and someone milk. Sachimaa boiled the bottle-gourd in milk. Mahaprabhu ate them. He met all other devotee-friends with Samkirtan and discussion on Lord Sri Krishna. Gadadhar Pundit and Haridas slept nearer to the place where Mahaprabhu slept.

Matrivandana

At first He worshipped mother Sachidevi saying - Mom, my dear mother, you have done for me lot. This body is your award to me. I never could serve for you. I just received your affection and results of your good qualities. I know I shall not be able to repay your debt in life after life. I shall remain indebted to you for ever. I know in this mortal world we come here for a few days and after some time we go back to Him. So please do not mind. Before it happens I am going for Sannyas, please Mom do not mind. I assure you will have no problem mother. Lord Sri Krishna will look after you all the time. Take it granted as the wishes of God Lord Sri Krishna. Dear mother please allow me to go. Do not get worried for me. Good bye Mom, good bye."

Sannyas at Katwa

Although Gadadhar and Haridas slept near His room but did not take them with Him and much before the dawn Gouranga Mahaprabhu set for Katwa alone advising them to meet next day at Katwa. Gouranga Mahaprabhu walked and crossed the Ganga river by swimming. At last reached Katwa. As he advised the associates like Sri Nityananda, Sri Gadadhar, Sri Haridas, Mukunda, Chandrasekhar and Brahmananda came over there. Then Keshab Bharati reached the place. Other people, devotees or non-devotees, assembled around Mahaprabhu. The barber sat to abolish the tuft, that indicates a symbol of a Brahmin, first then to shave the beautiful hair of Sri Gouranga Mahaprabhu.

The people gathered around Sri Gouranga and other associates cried a lot. They were stunned to see that such a young and nice looking strong and stout man is taking ascetic position. They including the barber and also the associates started to cry loudly. However, Gourangadev is Gourangadev. With tears in his eyes the barber abolished the tuft the symbol of Brahminism. Gouranga Mahaprabhu wanted to abolish caste system that prevailed for a long years and made the society crippled. He did not prefer any differences in human beings. After totally shaved the hair Gouranga Mahaprabhu was awarded initiation for asceticism from Keshab Bharati and He was given the name as Sri Krishnachaitanya, the Conscious of Lord Sri Krishna and the person who made others conscious about Lord Sri Krishna. It was a justified name for Him.

The Upsurge

We must admit that the mankind got back their consciousness that they are human beings, they have lot of things, and they need not be frustrated with the rulings of brute rulers. They started to work in their respective fields and to get peace and pleasure in uttering the name of God Lord Sri Krishna without causing any harm to anything in the world. All these changes and rejuvenation were possible only for the movement of Krishna naam started and led by Lord Sri Chaitanya.

With Desire of Yatra for Vrindavan

Sri Chaitanyadev with chanting the name of Lord Sri Krishna started to run towards the west to reach Vrindavan. The associates, who were present in Katwa like Nityananda, Gadadhar, Mukunda, Gobinda, and also the preceptor Keshab Bharati followed Him. All were engaged in dancing and chanting the songs for Lord Sri Krishna.

Through Western Area of Bengal

He reached the Rarh area of Bengal adjacent of Bihar now Jharkhand. The month approaching Falguna is the first part of the Spring when flowers palas, semul with their fire red colour decorate western part of Bengal. Other trees are also with different colours of flowers. Really the Spring gives joy to everyone with sweet breeze that carries fragrance of the nature. With nature's beauty and environment Sri Chaitanyadev felt the essence of Lord Sri Krishna and began Kirtan the chanting of songs for Lord Sri Krishna. All present and some of the villagers including children took part in songs and dances.

Chaitanyadev went just eight miles away from Bakreswar and then started to take journey towards the east with all the people gathered around Him with chanting Hare Krishna Naam and reached near the place where Ganga flows. Nityananda was sent to Adwyaitacharya at Shantipur that Mahaprabhu will be there soon.

Fulia, the Place of Haridas

Chaitanyadev came over Fulia (some say Kuliya), the place of Haridas. There also thousands of people including those who were physically handicapped flocked together and all got His darshan and felt themselves fortunate. Mahaprabhu Sri Chaitanyadev had the name of Lord Sri Krishna in the lips and tears for God in the eyes.

Mahaprabhu reached near the bank of the Ganga opposite side of Shantipur and bathed in the water considering the river as Ymuna, where on the bank in the divine forest Vrindavan Lord Sri Krishna played the eternal Lila.

He recited sloka for Yamuna -

"Chidanandabhaanoh Sadananda Suno Parama
Premgatri Draba Brahmagatri
Aghanang Labitri Jagatkshemdhatri Pabitri
Kriyanno Bapurmitraputri".

Shantipur

Sri Chaitanyadev stepped into the house of Sri Adwyaitacharya. Devotees from near and far assembled there too. At the entrance Mahaprabhu found the child son of Adwyaitacharya playing on dust and He took him in His arms with love. On the other side, Nityananda at

Nabadwip somehow could make Mother Sachidevi understand to leave the fasting she had for separation of lovely son. Sri Nityanandaprabhu brought Mother Sachidevi to the house of Sri Adwyaitacharya. All of the residents of Nabadwip and the mother were shocked to find their Gouranga Mahaprabhu shaved but they consoled themselves that Mahaprabhu now is again visible to them. The house became full with chanting Krishna naam and songs on Lord Sri Krishna.

10

ON WAY TO NEELACHAL

Mahaprabhu Chaitanyadev now is on the way of Neelachal i.e. Puri where the Temple of Lord Jagannath is gloriously situated. He was accompanied by the associates Nityananda, Gadadhar, Mukunda, Gobinda, Jagadananda, Brahmananda and some others. They walked through the district of 24 Parganas by the eastern side of the Ganga. Across Chhatrabhog, Mathurapur, Andhamuni etc. places he decided to reach Puri.

Chhatrabhog

Chhatrabhog is also a place of Shiva. Under the water there is established Shiva as Ambulinga. Mahaprabhu gave hearty respect to Ambulinga and made all the people there happy by performing Kirtan and dances with all the devotees present.

Ramchandra Khan

Here Ramchandra Khan (originally, Ghosh of Bally, near Uttarpara, Hooghly) was a devotee and by profession he was a wealthy and trustworthy owner of a Suba, representative of Hussain Shah. His area was not a small. Once somehow Ramchandra Khan failed to pay the taxes due and so he was imprisoned into the jail of the Ruler.

His relatives collected lot of money to pay up for his release. Ramchandra Khan understood that the amount so accumulated would not be sufficient for releasing a zeminder of big areas like him. He advised to deposit the whole amount in the treasury in favour of other zeminders of smaller areas and whose dues were lesser. Within a few days many small zeminders were released as their dues have been paid up. This incidence drew the attention of the Sultan Hussain Shah and he was surprised to note the benevolence Ramchandra Khan had shown. Hussain Shah waived the dues and awarded him with a title Mahasay (Sir, Khan). Since then his power and influence escalated.

There Sri Chaitanyadev with the associates and the villagers engaged in Samkirtan, all danced and sang the songs for Lord Sri Krishna. Ramchandra Khan arranged a boat for Chaitanyadev and the devotees to reach Orissa. All of the devotees including Sri Chaitanya Mahaprabhu started to sing and dance on the boat. The boat was about to sink and so the sailor requested them not to sing loudly lest their sound could reach the ears of dacoits and if they come they shall not spare them but to loot all their belongings and kill all by throwing into the water. At that time the political and administrative situation on both sides of Bengal and Orissa was much tensed. There was nobody to care and to look after the safety of passers-by in the borders.

Remuna

However Sri Chaitanyadev arrived Remuna where the

temple of Khirchora Gopinath is situated. It is heard that once the Deity himself had stolen one pot of Khir (delicious condensed sweet made of milk) from the twelve pots. Gopinath Himself as a boy went to Madhabendra Puri and offered the Khir Bhog to the hungry devotees Madhabendra Puri and his disciple Iswarpuri. So, Gopinath was called Khirchora Gopinath.

To see the Gopinath Deity Mahaprabhu Chaitanyadev sang songs and danced with all the associates and lost His senses with love for Lord Sri Krishna.

Jajpur a Place of Temples

Sri Chaitanyadev then arrived at Jajpur. There were innumerous temples of many deities of gods and goddesses at Jajpur. Alone Mahaprabhu roamed the place and everywhere He sang and danced in love for Lord Sri Krishna.

Sakshi Gopal

Then He reached Cuttack. There Mahaprabhu visited the Temple where the Deity of Sakshigopal remains. It is believed that Lord Sri Krishna from Vrindaban came Himself on foot in order to register His witness in favour of one of His devotees. The episode prevailing for long time, that one senior Brahmin on his pilgrimage became seriously ill and was left by villagers and relatives for die. Only one Brahmin boy bravely stayed, nursed and cured him. After complete healing the senior person being satisfied assured his junior company to get him married with his daughter. There was nobody who listened the words of assurances but the Deity of Gopal was in the temple. Gopal was considered as witness. Deity of Gopal started to move with the pilgrimage Brahmin boy on his way to return home but cautioned not to look back behind. The Brahmin boy crossed miles after miles but did not to look back for a while. They entered Orissa and the boy was almost nearer to his residence and for a while he wanted to be sure whether the black stone Deity is really walked and still walking with him for standing as a witness for him. Alas, the Deity stopped the journey and stood there as a stone made Deity of Lord Sri Krishna. Mahprabhu Sri Chaitanyadev recollected the episode and cried in love of God.

Bhubaneswar

Mahprabhu Sri Chaitanyadev bowed at every Shiva Temple; there He chanted the songs on Lord Sri Krishna and Shiva Pranam.

We may recollect once Poet Jayadev of Kenduli village on the bank of the Ajoy river a poet of the court of Raja Lakshman Sen was also a regular worshipper of Kusheswar Shiva. Sri Nityananda was also a worshipper of Lord Shiva at Ekchakra village in the district of Birbhum.

Kamalpur

Mahprabhu reached Kamalpur and from distance found the top of the Jagannath Temple. Mahaprabhu became almost mad to find the top of the Temple where Lord Sri Krishna remains as Jagannath, with Balaram and

Subhadra. With uttering the name of Lord Sri Krishna Mahaprabhu ran towards the temple alone and reached there.

In the Temple of Jagannath Prabhu

He wanted to touch the Deity of Lord Jagannath in order to embrace the Lord but the guards refused to allow Him to do it in the Temple. Mahaprabhu fainted and fell on the floor in love for God. The guards were about to beat Mahaprabhu. Fortunately, Sarbabhoum Bhattacharya, influential pundit, trusted personality of the King of Orissa was present there, and he somehow saved the life and arranged to carry the fainted body of Lord Sri Chaitanya to his house. Nityananda, Gadadhar, Mukunda, Jagadananda, Brahmananda and other devotees came, knew the situation, bowed at the main entrance of the Temple and rushed to the house of Sarbabhoum where Mahaprabhu was taken.

Sarbabhoum

Sarbabhoum Bhattacharya was some years senior to Mahaprabhu in age. He learnt the Nyayashastra in Mithila. At the time of return home in Bengal he was forbidden to carry any book with him. Before the appearance of Lord Gouranga Sarbabhoum with his talent and extra ordinary memory opened a school of Nyayashastra, thus with the efforts of Sarbabhoum,

---

**By Shri Radhakrishna Goswami (Radhu Goswami)*

Raghunath Siromani, Jagadish Pundit and others the place Nabadwip became an important centre of learning Nyayashastra. He was regarded as the 'prime pundit' of the whole country and abroad.

Therefore, he wanted to give some lessons on Adwyaitbad to this young and talented Sannyasi. Sri Chaitanyadev has shown immense patience in the class of seven days. He did not speak a single word. To see Sri Chaitanya's silence throughout the classes he assuming all the things he taught in the classes were not apprehensible, asked the student the reason behind this. Sri Chaitanyadev humbly answered that He did not prefer the narration without devotion to God Lord Sri Krishna.

Sarbabhoum became stunned and ultimately by leaving behind the way of Logic and teachings of Vedanta, he dived into the world of devotion. He felt Chaitanyadev as the Puranpurush Lord Vishnu. He understood that Lord Sri Krishna has appeared on this world to preach Bhakti the devotion towards God. He started to consider Sri Chaitanya as Lord Sri Krishna Himself. To him Sri Chaitanya and Jagannath - Balaram is one and same. It is heard later he himself drawn a sketch of six handed Sri Chaitanya in the Temple of Lord Jagannath.

The news of Sarbabhoum's participation in the movement with Sri Chaitanyadev with invisible wings reached the corners of the States of Bengal and Orissa and other part of the Country

The Devotees of Orissa

The people of Orissa from villages and towns came to Puri to see Lord Sri Chaitanyadev and many of them joined the team of Samkirtan. Among them Pradyumna Mishra, Premanada, Ramananda, Damodar Pundit, Srisankar, Pradyumna Brahmachari, Bhagaban Acharya became associates of Lord Sri Chaitanyadev. Thus within a short time the pilgrimage Puri became full of Samkirtan with songs on Lord Sri Krishna by Sri Chaitanyadev and His associates of Bengal and Orissa. Mahaprabhu spent two months including the participation in the Dolyatra Festival there.

11

MAHAPRABHU TRAVELED SOUTH INDIA

It is a matter of surprise and beyond our imagination that alone Sri Chaitanyadev wandered miles on bare foot by chanting and dancing for Love for Lord Sri Krishna a 500 years ago. Then roads on His way were through forests and hills and many rivers. Sri Chaitanyadev decided to trek towards the south. In the next Baisakh He started His journey. He decided to go alone but others raised objection that alone Mahaprabhu should not walk because sometimes He is fainted in love for God Lord Sri Krishna and He would need at least one man to hold His clothes and water pot. At last all decided to send a man named Krishnadas for this job. Gadadhar Pundit His constant company has to remain in Puri with Kshetra Sannyas being engaged to worship Tota Gopinath, the Deity that Mahaprabhu revealed from beneath the sands of the sea beach of Puri. However all including Gadadhar, Nityananda went with Mahaprabhu Sri Chaitanyadev unto Alalnath and from there they bid fare well. Mahaprabhu then started to walk towards south to south. Krishnadas just tried to follow Mahaprabhu or the sounds of Songs sang by Lord Sri Chaitanya—

Krishna Krishna Krishna Krishna Krishna Krishna Krishnahe
Krishna Krishna Krishna Krishna Krishna Krishna Krishnahe
Krishna Krishna Krishna Krishna Krishna Krishna Rakshamum
Krishna Krishna Krishna Krishna Krishna Krishna Paahimum
Rama Raghava Rama Raghava Rama Raghava Rakshamum
Krishna Keshaba Krishna Keshaba Krishna Keshaba Paahimum.

Alalnath

Mahaprabhu went to Jagannathpur near the lake Chilka. There He lived in a house of a Brahamin gentleman. The house owner considered Him as Jagannath Himself. From then the place was called Jagannathpur. Then Mahaprabhu visited the Kurma place. Now it is called as Srikakulam. On the way of His running to Kurmasthan there was Shiva Temple of Mukhalingam Shiva. There Mahaprabhu sang and danced in honour of the master of Kurma Vishnu Swami. There Mahaprabhu met a vaidik brhamin person Kurma by name. He advised him to circulate the name of Lord Sri Krishna. It is also learnt here Mahaprabhu Sri Chaitanyadev pitied on a lepor. Then Mahaprabhu proceeded towards more souths and reached Simhachalam.

Simhachalam and the River Godavari

This place is called Jior Nrisingha Kshetra. There were one thousand stairs above the hill where the temple of Lakshmi Baraha Nrisinghadev is situated. With the name of Lord Sri Krishna, Mahaprabhu climbed the hill. After songs and dance in love for Lord Sri Krishna, he ran again towards more souths.

Roy Ramananda

Then crossed the Godavari River that called Goutami Ganga and reached Vidyanagar (Rajmahendri now called Rajmundri). Mahaprabhu was initially informed by Sarbabhoum Acharya of Puri of the fact that here resides Roy Ramananda who had deep knowledge in Lord Sri Krishna and had great devotion in Him. He was the principal ruler of the area on behalf of the king of Orissa. Therefore, at first appearance, he was a rich man with luxurious life style but internally he was a great devotee of Lord Sri Krishna.

Mahaprabhu Sri Chaitanyadev bathed in the river Godavari and sang the songs of Lord Sri Krishna and on the other hand Roy Ramananda with his royal team reached the ghat of the Godavari for taking his daily bath. Both of them recognized one another. They discussed the love of God and the love for God. There the Sadhya Sadhan Tattwa an important philosophy of Vaishnavism was established by Sri Chaitanyadev and Roy Ramananda and it took ten days. Thousands of people of different ideologies gathered around Sri Chaitanya for his sweet Kirtan and madly dance in the name of Lord Sri Krishna. Here people became attracted to Him as well as Lord Sri Krishna and they became Vaishnavas.

Other Shiva Temples

Mahaprabhu visited Koti Lingeswar Shiva Temple,

Markendaya Temple, Draksharam, Palkannu, Vimabharam, and a Shiva Temple at Antarvedi the all holy places there and duly worshipped the Deities with His melodious songs and madly dance for Lord Sri Krishna.

Nrisinghadev

Afterwards by passing Vijayawada and the river, the Krishnaa Mahaprabhu arrived at Mangalgiri on the lap of East Coast Mountains. There remains the Deity of Nrisingha whose main Bhog was Pana Sarbat a kind of beverage. He visited the Deity and also Rajalakshmi. He started kirtan and cited slokas. All the devotees there became enthusiastic.

Shrisailam

Then Mahaprabhu went to Sri Sailam. The way was on the side of the river Krishnaa and Mahaprabhu with Kirtan and dance advanced the path and reached Sri Sailam. Here He visited the Jyortilinga Mallikarjuna Mahadev Shiva Temple. There flows the river Krishnaa on three sides and the Temple is situated on the Rishava mountain. The surroundings were full of beauty of forests. Mahapraprabhu bathed in the river Krishnaa and recited Shiva stotras and passed some days there.

Abaloham

At southern part there He visited Dasaram Shiva Temple with same devotion. Mahaprabhu Sri Chaitanyadev walked on bare feet and almost bare body miles after miles only with the name of Lord Sri Krishna swinging in the lips. It appears that the entire universe is listening the name Lord Sri Krishna in the lips of Mahaprabhu. Mahaprabhu visited all other Temples including the Temple of Nrisinghadev.

Siddhoibat

Then Mahaprabhu reached Siddhoibat through Pushpagiri. He visited the Temple of Raghunathji and worshipped there Sri Ramchandra and thereafter sang the songs for Lord Sri Krishna that made all of the area charmed. Many became devotees of Lord Sri Krishna too.

Tirujani

At Tirujani Skandadev, known as Subrahmnyadev, the commander-in-chief of the gods and goddesses Kartikeya's Temple is on the high altitude of a hill. Mahaprabhu Sri Chaitanyadev did not care the stiff stairs of the hill and reached the Temple to offer due respect.

Then He proceeded at Trimalla to visit the Trivikram.

Sri Kaalhasti-Briddha Kasi

Mahaprabhu Sri Chaitanyadev reached Sri Kaalhasti-Briddha Kasi and worshipped with regards the Shiva Linga Sri Kaal Hastiswar. It is inside of a cave where no wind can enter into and a mere lamp is inflaming and shivering. Very near Mahaprabhu remained.

Obstacles on the Ways

Some of the orthodox dispassionate Brahmin

challenged Him. Mahaprabhu had left the habit of debating long before in His early years' Vidyavilas stage. However, Mahaprabhu was not a personality of being defeated at ease. He also succeeded to win over logics cited by some Buddhist monk. Indeed Mahaprabhu Sri Chaitanyadev was an extra ordinary talented rare personality in this world ever. Now at ease Mahaprabhu conquered them, some fled and some of them became Vaishnava with pleasure.

No, Mahaprabhu Sri Chaitanyadev did not bother any obstacles. The paths were not easy to cover on bare feet. There were natural hinderances like rains, storms, the scorching sunrays, flooded rivers, the roads, the hills, the bushes and forests, the beasts with sharp nails and teeth, the people who tried to oppose and even the greedy miscreants.

However, Mahaprabhu Sri Chaitanyadev could overcome on all the obstacles in the path of Kirtan of Lord Sri Krishna. Language problem could not hinder Mahaprabhu Sri Chaitanyadev because all could realize the songs for God Lord Sri Krishna. He had Sri Krishna in the heart, Sri Krishna in the lips, love for Lord Sri Krishna in the whole of His surroundings and love for the mankind irrespective of religion, country, colour, caste, creed, languages whatever differences were and are. You can imagine and feel in your heart that before more than five hundred years ago there was present Mahaprabhu. A tall fair almost bare body walked miles after miles by raising the two long hands high up only by shedding tears and uttering songs for love for God Lord Sri Krishna in all the seasons in all the paths by seaside, riverside, through dense forests, the hills.

With Sri Krishna in the lips, He walked towards more souths.

Thirupati-Thirumalai

Then Sri Chaitanyadev arrived at Thirupati-Thirumalai. It was named Tripadi-Thrimalla. He visited the Vishnu idol with four hands at Venkatachalam. Covered the stairs and visited many Temples with due respect there. Underneath there remains the Deity of Tirupati, Vishnu. There He offered His devotion and wandered other Temples. At Swami Kodandaram's Temple of Raghunath, Ramchandra, He praised God with stotras, sang songs, and danced for God.

Kanchipuram

Afterwards He reached at Kanchipuram where Shiva as Ekambareswar Maheswar stays as Kshiti, the world. He duly worshipped there. Sri Chaitanyadev visited other Shiva Temples and at Kamkothipith the goddess Kamakshi. He offered respect and devotion. Here thousands of people started to become Vaishnavas.

Shivakanchi

At Shivakanchi, there is Baradraaj Vishnu Temple and other Deities' Temples. He worshipped the Deities with honour and many people became Vaishnavas. All these were possible for His Love for mankind and for God, God

Sri Krishna. Then He visited Arunachaleswar Tejolinga Shiva at Thiruvanna Malai.

Mahabalipuram

Then Mahaprabhu Sri Chaitanyadev reached Mahabalipuram, earlier known as Trikaalhasti. The holy place is also called Pakshi Tirtham as two birds come there regularly at the lunch time after taking Prasadam they fly towards unknown place for the last hundreds of years. There He visited Vedgiriswar Shiva Mahadev and Parbati, the mother.

Chidambaram

At Chidambaram, after Briddhakol and white Baraha Temple He arrived Yellow dressed Shiva place and worshipped Shiva in the shape of the sky. There flows the river Cauveri, the Goutami Ganga, that was brought form Kailash by the sage Agasthya and flown by Shiva-Parbati nandan Bal Ganesha.

Having crossed the river Cauveri Mahaprabhu Sri Chaitanyadev walked and walked towards more souths. After Thiruvayur He entered the Vedavan, Vedaranyam and found the beauty of the forest and also the Bay of Bengal came in His sight. There live some ancient sages. Giving proper love He paid respect to them and the Deity of Shiva in the Temple. Mahaprabhu Sri Chaitanyadev went some western side of seashore and reached Tanjor. There at Gangaikonda Cholpuram He worshipped the Amritalinga Shiva and Brihadiswar Shiva and inspired other devotees in the mantra of Love, Love for mankind and Love for God, Lord Sri Krishna.

Kumbhakonam

Then he reached at Kumbhakonam, early known as Kumbha Karma Kapaal. There is Mahamaghav lake and Kumbheswar Shiva. Mahaprabhu visited the temple and other temples of Vishnu and Hanuman. After worshipping there with devotion, Sri Chaitanyadev proceeded to Papnashan and then to Srirangam.

Srirangam

On the bank of the river there is the biggest Vishnu temple situated in Srirangam placed in an island in between the Cauveri and its branch river Kollidam. It is heard that once upon a time there were seven boundary walls around the place Srirangam. It is also known that Acharya Sri Ramanuja had started Vaishnavism from Srirangam. Here Sri Chaitanyadev decided to stay the four months for observing the Chaturmasya at the request of Sri Venkata Bhatta of Sri sect. His son Gopal Bhatta was engaged to look after Sri Chaitanyadev. Thousands of devotees requested Mahaprabhu to receive alms from their houses but Sri Chaitanyadev was unable to receive everybody's alms as the number of days (around 120 days in 4 months) was much less than the number of persons who opted to offer at least one day's alms.

Reading the Gita

Here Mahaprabhu, found a devotee with simple dress

and appearance reading loudly the Gita daily at the portico of the temple. It seemed that the reader of the Gita had no sufficient background of education, neither he could pronounce correctly the words written in Sanskrit but while reading, he was charmed himself. Others may ignore or neglect him as a laughingstock but Sri Chaitanyadev noticing his state of being overwhelmed with emotion asked why he cries or laughs or keeps quiet sometime during his regular reading. He replied that he sees Lord Sri Krishna while in reading. Lord Sri Krishna is holding the ropes of the chariot of Arjuna and tells the slokas of the Gita to Arjuna. This scene becomes clear to him and so he cannot resist himself of crying, laughing or keeping quiet for sometime. Mahaprabhu noticed that people coming there give a sight of negligence and do not halt for a single moment to listen the reading. So, He told him not to care other people who ignore him and the unpolished reading. He is the right person to read the Gita as Lord Sri Krishna Himself comes down to him. Not only just reading but to feel in heart is the best thing Mahaprabhu Sri Chaitanyadev advised the person there.

Gopal Bhatta

To see Gopal Bhatta's deep devotion in the service at Venkata Bhatta's house Mahaprabhu advised him to worship Lord Sri Krishna at Vrindavan and to take some charges of His work at Vrindavan. Afterwards this Gopal Bhatta in Vrindavan took shelter of Sri Sanatan and Sri Roop. There he worshipped Salagram Lord Sri Krishna in belief of Sri Chaitanyadev's assurance that one day he would have a darshan of Lord Sri Krishna. It is told that the Deity of Sri Sri Radharaman was appeared from this Salagram. There he wrote *Haribhakti Vilas,* a detailed guidebook of Vaishnavism and became one of the Six Goswamis of Vrindavan.

Trichinapalli

At Trichinapalli, earlier known as Tiruchirapalli, Mahaprabhu visited the temple of Vinayaka, the Ganesha Deity and worshipped with profound devotion.

More South on Way to Kanyakumari

Now after the Chaturmasya Sri Chaitanyadev moved more the south to the last point of India Kanyakumari with the name of Sri Krishna in the lips :

Krishna Krishna Krishna Krishna Krishna Krishna Krishnahe
Krishna Krishna Krishna Krishna Krishna Krishna Krishnahe
Krishna Krishna Krishna Krishna Krishna Krishna Rakshamum
Krishna Krishna Krishna Krishna Krishna Krishna Paahimum
Rama Raghava Rama Raghava Rama Raghava Rakshamum
Krishna Keshaba Krishna Keshaba Krishna Keshaba Paahimum.

Sri Shaila

Sri Chaitanyadev on His way to Kanyakumari found hundreds of Temples and at every Temple paid due respect. Mahaprabhu Sri Chaitanyadev reached Sri Shaila where He found a Brahmin couple and recognized them as Lord Shiva and Parvati. They also recognized Mahaprabhu as Lord Sri Krishna. All became overwhelmed.

Dakshin Mathura

Then Mahaprabhu went to Puri Kamkosthi and from there to Dakshin Mathura. There lived Ramdas a devotee of Sri Ramchandra and Mahaprabhu accepted his invitation for alms. But surprisingly He noticed that Ramdas only thinking of Lord Sri Ramchandra during all the time and made no arrangement of cooking for himself or Sri Mahaprabhu till the midday. He asked the reason. Ramdas replied that Lakshman has gone into the deep forest to collect fruits and other vegetables and after return Sita mother will cook. But alas the rakshas king Ravana has taken away mother Sitadevi. Rakshas has touched the holy mother Sitadevi and so living by taking food has no meaning to him. It was an impossible matter to make understand such a devotee of Sri Ram, however Sri Chaitanyadev told him :

"Ishwarpreyasi Sita Chidananda Murti,
Prakrita Indriye Taren Dekhite Nari.
And He said again,
Aprakrita Bastu Nahe Prakrita Gochar,
Veda Puranete ei Kahe Nirantar".

Sitadevi is loved by Lord and Herself is the Chidanada and with earthly eyes we cannot see Her. She is beyond to touch and She is ever with us. Ravana could only take the shadow Sita away. The devotee should repent and he should take prasadam daily to live in this world otherwise he would die in starvation.

Durbeshan

After taking bath at Kritamalay Mahaprabhu went to

Durbeshan and visited the Temple of Raghunathji i.e. Sri Ramchandra.

Mahendra Hill

At Mahendra hill He paid respect to Parshuram. He went to Setubandha and bathed at Dhonu Pilgrim and in Ramaswar visited the Temple and decided to take a pause for listening the Kurma Purana that supported His saying what He consoled Ramdas at south Mathura earlier. He copied the explanation portion Himself and again returned to Dakshin Mathura to show Ramdas the devotee of Sri Ramchandra.

सीतयाराधितो बह्निच्छाया सीतमजी जनत्।
तं जहार दशग्रीबाः सीता बह्निपुरः गता।।
परीक्षासमये बह्निं छायासीता बिबशे सा।
बह्नि सीतां समानीय तत्पुरुशस्तादनीनयत्।।-कुर्म पुराण

Sityaradhito banhichchhaya sitamaji janat.
Twant jahara Dashagribah Sita banhipurah gata.
Pariksha samaye banhing chhaya Sita bibasa saa.
Banhi Situng Sumuniyu tutpurustuduneenuyut.

Here Ramdas started to consider Sri Chaitanyadev as his Sri Ramchandra. He was delighted and it cannot be measured.

Tamraparni in Pandyasthan

From there, Sri Chaitanyadev reached Tamraparni in Pandyasthan. He visited the Temples of Sri Ramchandra and Lakshman at Tilkanchi (Tenkanchi) Shiva Viswanath and Parvati, at Gajendra Pilgrim near Nagarkoil Sri

Vishnu Temple, Temple at Panagarih, at Temples of Ramchandra and Vishnu at Totadri and other temples of Shiva, Kartikeya. Everywhere He distributed Love for God and Mankind so that all the people can love each other and everyone's God of any belief everyone possesses.

Near Rishava hill He worshipped the sage Agasthya. There Mahaprabhu found Paramanandapuri who just completed the Chaturmasya and both of them embraced one another. Mahaprabhu invited him to meet him in Neelachal in near future.

Kanyakumari

Then Mahaprabhu arrived at Kanyakumari, at the last south point of India. There are oceans like the Bay of Bengal on the east, the Indian Ocean to the south and the Arabian Sea to the west on three sides. At first Sri Chaitanyadev took bath at the pond Papa Vinashan at north of the temple. Then He bathed at the scheduled place in the sea where water of three seas mix. There remains the temple of Vinayaka. It is told that Indra, the Dev Raj has built the temple of Vinayaka. Towards the east on the side of Bay of Bengal there are Temples of Savitri, Gayatri, Saraswati, Kanya and Vinayaka. On the sides of Indian Ocean the pilgrim places of Mother, Father and Bhima. On the western side the pilgrim place of Sthanu, the stagnant. (Here now a statue of Bapuji Mahatma Gandhi has been erected). Here is a mandapam with sixteen pillars where rites for ancestors can be observed.

It is learnt that the goddess Mahamaya, the Shakti as a virgin girl is waiting with a garland in hands for Shiva, the Mahadeva. The goddess Shakti appeared this time there to destroy Banasura till virginity continues but if she is married to Shiva who would kill Banasura? In nobody's hand Banasura would die as it was a boon from Shiva. All the gods gathered their power for offering into burn to evolve the goddess Shakti this time that could only demolish the Banasura. It was a conspiracy of Narada to stop the marriage of eternal Mother and Father, Shakti and Shiva. Shiva in time taking coconut without eyes, sugar candy without knot and betal without any vein started the journey that to be completed before the dawn. On the eve of completion of journey of Shiva near Suchindram it was night and there had lot of time to rise the sun. Narada then from Vasukkamparoi the side of the virgin daughter sounded as a cock like an efficient Harbola artist. The condition was to reach with those uncommon materials before dawn. What will do Bholanath Shiva? He stood and stranded there thinking the night has ended and the dawn has approached. On the other side the goddess Shakti as a virgin daughter Kanyakumari remains for ever here. Sripadaparai,the sign of Shakti Kanyakumari still remains. It is told the Temples were built by Parsuram, then different kings at different times renovated the Temples. Sri Chaitanyadev worshipped, sang and danced with joy in love for God at the Temples there including Suchindram, the Temples of Brahma, Vishnu, Shiva and Hanumanji.

Vellimalai

At Vellimalai Mahaprabhu visited Tamal-Kartikeya Temple and worshipped there with melodious songs for Lord Sri Krishna. Near Nagarkoil at Bhutapondi now known as Betapani visited the Temple of Sri Ramchandra.

Then He entered the then Malabar area and accidentally, Sri Chaitanyadev met some Bhattamari devotees who could capture Krishnadas by luring greed for woman. Mahaprabhu Sri Chaitanyadev could easily defeat the gang and rescue the companion from their hands. We, the earthly men can hardly measure His beyond thinkable immense power.

Thiruvattura

Mahaprabhu Sri Chaitanyadev reached at Thiruvattura. He visited the Adi Keshaba Temple and sang for Lord Sri Krishna with all the people in emotion. He found the ancient scripture BRAHMA SAMHITA and read with devotion and copied the book that considered as the mines of experiences of ancient sages.

Thiruvanthapuram: Pediar-Payashwini

Then Mahaprabhu arrived at Trivandram, Thiruvanthapuram where Temple of Padmanava Vishnu Deity and other Temples exist. Through the western shore, now Mahaprabhu Sri Chaitanyadev started to run faster towards the north and after visiting Srinarkom reached Kaladi the birthplace of Sankaracharya and bathed at the river Pediar-Payashwini and sang, danced at the Sri Krishna Temple established by Sankaracharya. Here it should be mentioned that both the preceptors of Sri

Chaitanyadev, Ishwarpuri and Keshab Bharati were from Puri and Bharati branches created by Sankaracharya and so Mahaprabhu paid homage to Sankaracharya as the Chief Preceptor of Puri and Bharati branches.

Guruvaur-Calicut-Shringeri

Then He reached Guruvaur, then at Calicut and places on the bank of the river Tungabhadra and then to Shringeri Mutt of Sankaracharya. Thereafter arrived at the Temple of Bal Gopal established by Madhyacharya. Here also Mahaprabhu had to establish Bhaktidharma the religion of Love and Devotion after some debates with local worshippers. He sang from Srimadbhagawata - (7/5/23 & 24)

"Shravanam Kirtanam Vishno Smaranam Paadsevanam
Archanam Vandanam Dasyang Sakshyamatmanivedanam
Eti Pungsaarpita Vishnoi Bhaktischennablakshmana
Kriyate Bhagabatyadhwa Tonmoneyhadhilamullamam."

That expresses (as Prahlad suggested father Hiranyakashipu) that if a devotee who considers worshipping the Lord Sri Krishna he should have the nine qualities of Listening, Singing for God, Remembering, Serving at the Feet of Lord, Worshipping, Praising, becoming a Servant, Friendly and Surrendering everything even oneself completely to Him is the best way of pleasing Lord Sri Krishna and that is the best learning.

Udipi

From Sringeri Mutt Sri Chaitanyadev reached Udipi, the birth place of Madhyacharya. Here Mahaprabhu was confronted also with some devotees and easily He could convince them the Bhakti Marg, the way of devotion.

Bellur Tritakupa

Then Sri Chaitanya Mahaprabhu came to Bellur Tritakupa the Falgu pilgrim. It is situated towards the east of Udipi. He visited the Temples of Channakeshab and others and became overwhelmed to find the art of the Temples.

Jog Falls-Panchapsara

Then arrived at the Panchapsara, the Jog Falls in the Sahyadri Range in the Western Hills. Once in the age of Mahabharata the third Pandava Arjuna took his bath and with his touch five cursed nymphs of Paradise in the shape of crocodiles got back their earlier forms. Sri Chaitanya Mahaprabhu took a bath and offered water to the manes. The place is in the deep forests and hills. The water is still falling in four streams from around one thousand feet high to a big ditch. Even to day one may be horrified to visit the spot, possibly the biggest water falls in the south-east Asia.

Gokarna

In the same Sahyadri Range in the Western Hills there is Gokarna island in the Arabian Sea where Deity of Lord Shiva exists, Sri Chaiyanyadev worshipped with high regards.

Pottakadal

Then Sri Chaiyanyadev reached Pottakadal, Surparak pilgrim and got immense delight to find the artistic sculptures. From here Sri Chaitanya Mahaprabhu went to Kohlapur and visited the Temples of Ambaji, Mahalakshmi, Bhabani the mother, Langa Ganeshji and of others.

Saint Tukaram

After this He went to Pandharpur the birth place of Saint Tukaram. It is learnt that Saint Tukaram once also became fond of Vaishnavism. On the bank of the river Bhima or Bhimarathi and visited the Deity of fourhanded Sri Narayana as named Vitthaldeva or Vidhobadeva there. He sang and danced in love for God Lord Sri Krishna. Here Sri Chaitanya Mahaprabhu came across Srirangapuri one of the disciples of Madhabendrapuri. Mahaprabhu was disciple of Ishwarpuri who was also a disciple of Madhabendrapuri and so Srirangapuri was in the level of preceptor of Sri Chaitanya Mahaprabhu and He offered due respect to Srirangapuri.

Mahabaleswar

Then Sri Chaitanya Mahaprabhu ran towards north through the Sahyadri Range and reached Mahabaleswar nearer to the river Krishnachenwa or Krishnabenwa and worshipped Lord Vishnu and Lord Shiva at the Temples. He met some pious Vaishnavas here and listened oration of an unavailable scripture *SRIKRISHNA KARNAMRITA* once written by Billamangal and became overwhelmed in love for God Lord Sri Krishna. He arranged for writing of a copy of it.

Again He walked and walked miles after miles with chanting the name of Lord Sri Krishna and reached near the Tapti river. There took bath and sang for God. He came on the bank of the river Narmada and visited Mahimatipur, Omkarmandhata or Omkareswar then arrived Ujjain where Jyotirlinga Shiva remains in the Temple of Mahakaal. He took bath in the water of the rivers Narmada and also Nirvindhya.

Seven Palmyra Trees

He came over Rishyamuk hill, Dandyakaranya forest, Matangaashram and then at Dhanutirtha. There remained seven palmyra trees from the ages of the Ramayana. Once those were cut by Sri Ramchandra with one single arrow to show Sugrib His heavenly power for joining in the battle against Ravana who lifted mother Sita from the cottage made by Sri Ramchandra and Sri Laxmana in the forest. Mahaprabhu Sri Chaitanyadev embraced the trees standing in cut position for long long years back and as He touched them they all vanished within a moment. To see this uncommon thing people there started to sing praising the glory of Lord Sri Chaitanyadev. They, perhaps, considered Him as Sri Ramchandra Himself.

Then Sri Chaitanyadev took bath in the water of Pampa Lake and reached Panchabati. Here Sri Ramchandra and Sri Laxmana in the forest made a cottage and lived with Sita the mother during the time of their fourteen years' exile in forest. Lord Sri Chaitanyadev with due respect took rest and went to Nasik where Sri Laxmana was forced to hurt by cutting the nose of Surpanakha, sister of Ravana the King of Lanka.

He visited Jyortilinga Shiva at the Temple of Trambakya and went to Brahmagiri hill to visit the Kushabarta pilgrimage from where the river Godavari starts. He walked by the side of the bank as the Godavari runs in serpentine form through the forests full of wild animals.

Mahaprabhu at Other Places

It is also said by some writers that Sri Chaitanyadev visited Pune, the centre of education from ancient times, then Khandabat, Daman, Surat, Broch, Baroda and Dakor and again Baroda, Ahmedabad and crossed the river Sabarmoti or Subhramoti to reach Dwarka and on His way Somnath Temple. Then by the sides of the river the Narmada and the Godavari by passing through Dohad, Mandalnagar, Devghar, Shibaninagar, Malaya hills, Chandipur, Raipur and some other places he started to return. He received immense love and recognition from the places where He sang and danced in Love for Lord Sri Krishna. He had immense love for the People all everywhere.

The Return - Vidyanagar

At last after two years' vigorous journey on foot only Sri Chaitanya Mahaprabhu returned at Vidyanagar, the place of Roy Ramananda. Roy Ramananda with some waiting devotees rushed to Him and both embraced one and other. Sri Chaitanya Mahaprabhu gave the two unavailable scriptures *Brahmasamhita* and *Krishnakarnamrita* to Roy Ramananda who arranged to copy the Books.

Return to Neelachal

After seven days Sri Chaitanya Mahaprabhu decided to return to Neelachal where the Deity of Lord Jagannath remains with Balaram and Subhadra in the Temple. Pundit Gadadhar, Nityananda, Jagadananda, Damodar Pundit, Mukunda, Gopinath Acharya and other devotees all came to receive Him. Sarbabhoum Bhattacharya also reached the Sea-shore to receive Him cordially and they embraced each other.

Krishnadas having been released from duty rushed to Nabadwip to meet mother Sachidevi to give her the news that after completing tour in the south, Sri Chaitanyadev has returned to Puri, Neelachal.

Neelachal the place of Lord Jagannath is in the heart of people of Orissa and Bengal and of all the states of India for pilgrimage and also for the beautiful Sea Beach, now the place has got an additional attraction for Lord Sri Chaitanyadev.

He sang and danced glorifying God Lord Sri Krishna-Lord Jagannath there.

12

VISIT IN GOUD BENGAL

After a few days He decided to come back to Bengal for having a bath in the water of the river Ganga and visit some places. Thousands of devotees and ordinary people of Goud Bengal were eagerly awaiting the safe return of Sri Chaitanya Mahaprabhu from the vast South India.

The accompanying team was comprised with Ramananda, Paramananda Puri, Swarup Damodar, Jagadananda, Gobinda, Bakreswar, Mukunda and other followers. Here Sri Chaitanyadev did not take His associate from infancy Gadadhar but Gadadhar started to walk with loving friend Sri Chaitanya Mahaprabhu because it was decided that Sri Chaitanya Mahaprabhu would go to Mathura-Vrindavan after visiting Bengal and the river Ganga.

Gadadhar Mahima (glory)

His infancy-long associate Gadadhar cannot let Sri Chaitanyadev go alone to Mathura-Vrindavan. Once Gadadhar allowed Sri Chaitanyadev for South India tour for long period of two years and now it would be difficult for him to live for a single day without seeing and serving Sri Chaitanya Mahaprabhu. Sri Chaitanyadev wanted to convince him to stay in Puri with the worshipping of Tota

Gopinath, the deity recovered from under the sand of the sea beach. He tried to console Gadadhar that to serve Tota Gopinath will be sufficient as he used to and liked to serve Mahaprabhu. But Gadadhar Pundit was like an unyielding child and at last he said - O.K., I'm going alone to see Sachimaa in Goud Bengal. I shall choose a separate path'. Mahaprabhu Sri Chaitanyadev could not speak a single word against this topic as He Himself was feeling thirst to see the Mother, the Motherland and the Mother River Ganga but He was full of anxiety for lone traveler Gadadhar and the worshipping of Tota Gopinath. And from way at Cuttack He called for Gadadhar Pundit back and told him-"I understand your extreme happiness to be with me but it will be a cause of my sorrow if you give up your duty for some days also. I hope you do not want to see me in a condition of sorrow for you. If you want my pleasure please go back Neelachal."

Vidyabachaspati's House

Sri Chaitanyadev returned to Bengal after crossing Panihati, Kumarhatta (Halsahar), Kanchanpalli (Kanchrapara), and then reached and decided to stay there where Vidyabachaspati one son of Maheswar Visharad resides. We can remember the another son of Visharad was Sarbabhoum of Neelachal. There Mahaprbhu took bath in the water of the river Ganga and wanted to stay only by chanting the name of Lord Sri Krishna lonely for a few days and thereafter He could start journey for Vrindavan-Mathura.

However the news of His stay there was spread all over Bengal within a short period and thousands of people from different corners started to assemble together there to have a glimpse of Lord Sri Chaitanyadev. Some came also by swimming in the river Ganga as all the boats were overloaded each time while crossed the river. Mahaprabhu preferred a solitary place to take rest and chant the name of Lord Sri Krishna before expected journey to Mathura-Vrindavan. To see the unthinkable crowd accumulated everyday, one day with some of His followers went to Kuliya at the house of Madhabdas Chattopadhyay. The assembled people did not believe it and thought that it is nothing but a trick of Vidyabachaspati to have the scope of serving Sri Chaitanyadev alone and so he has kept hidden Chaitanyadev inside the house. They shouted and told him to show at least one appearance of Sri Chaitanyadev to quench the thirst of the eyes of the people. Within a few days knowing the truth Vidyabachaspati with all the people rushed to Kuliya to have a darshan of Lord Sri Chaitanyadev.

Mahaprabhu forgave Gopal Chapal through Sribaas met Bakreswar Pundit, tantrik Krishnananda and many followers. There came Devananda Pundit who used to read and teach the Srimad Bhagabata to listeners and students. Mahaprabhu explained to him that without devotion *BHAKTI* the Bhagabata should not be read out to everyone. The eternal love cannot be discussed everywhere to any person without Bhakti.

Sri Chaitanyadev at Ramkeli

Ramkeli is nearer to the capital of Goud Bengal ruler Hussain Shah and on the bank of the river Ganga. Thousands of people irrespective of caste and creed and religion including street beggars and lepor knew the presence of Lord Sri Chaitanyadev and all flocked together there to have a glimpse. The place became full of Samkirtan of the name of Lord Sri Krishna whole day and night. Hussain Shah came to know the news. He sent Keshab Khan, an employee of the King's Court to confirm the fact. He after seeing Mahaprabhu and His emotion in devotion of Lord Sri Krishna all the time came back and advised Hussain Shah it would be better not to disturb the monk from whom no sign of any danger for the kingdom is expected. There came Roop and Sanatan. They were named as Dabir Khas and Sagir Mullick by the ruler Hussain Shah. Their original names were Santosh and the elder Amar. Mahaprabhu gave Dabir Khas and Sagir Mullick names as Roop and Sanatan. Sri Roop advised Sri Chaitanyadev not to start for Mathura Vrindavan as the roads may not be favourable for tour and also not to stay nearer to the Capital assuming variable moods of the King.

Achyutananda, Five Years' Old Son of Adwyaitacharya

Now Sri Chaitanyadev started to return to Puri the place of Lord Jagannath. His journey on foot towards Neelachal-Puri was by the side of the river Ganga and He reached the house of Adwyaitacharya at Shantipur. Five years' old child of Adwyaitacharya, Achyutananda greeted Mahaprabhu first and He took him in His arms. In later days this child became a disciple of Gadadhar Pundit and an important personality among the followers of Lord Sri Chaitanyadev.

Sachimaa

Adwyaitacharya arranged to bring Sachidevi the Mother from Nabadwip to Shantipur. Then Sachimaa was like a lunatic woman as she questioned everyone she meets the different situation of Lord Sri Krishna at Mathura. To see Mother at Adwyaitacharya's house then and there Sri Chaitanyadev fell at the feet of Mother Sachidevi and confessed that no one can pay up the debts of a mother. She took the charge of cooking for Sri Chaitanyadev and prepared various items of fry and shak and other vegetables as Mahaprabhu Sri Chaitanyadev preferred. After Shantipur Mahaprabhu Sri Chaitanyadev arrived at Sri Baas's house at Kumarhatta.

Mahaprabhu at Sri Baas's House at Kumarhatta

Here Ishwarpuri was born. Sri Baas expressed his tremendous joy to have Sri Chaitanyadev at his residence. There came father-like Purandar Acharya, came Basudev Dutta, Sibananda Sen and many other devotees and followers. All made the house full of Samkirtan. Sri Chaitanyadev praised highly Basudev Dutta and Ramai Pundit. Here Mahaprabhu noticed the poor pecuniary condition of Sri Baas. As Sri Baas cannot ask for anything of livelyhood from anybody or to go outside for earning. He preferred to stay at home and to sing for Lord Sri Krishna and Lord Sri Chaitanyadev the whole of the days. Mahaprabhu Sri Chaitanyadev advised Ramai and other followers to look after Sri Baas so that he can chant the name of God without having any anxiety for earning bread and clothes for the other members of the family. All agreed to look after this aspect and gave assurance to Mahaprabhu Sri Chaitanyadev. Mahaprabhu could realize this hard reality and tried to solve the problems with other fellowmen.

Panihati

Mahaprabhu alongwith the followers arrived at Panihati on the bank of the river Ganga (near the Railway station Sodepur). Here resides Raghav Pundit. Getting Mahaprabhu suddenly at his house Raghav Pundit became overwhelmed with joy and devotion.

Mahaprabhu told all there-

"Gangayay majjan koiley ye santosh hai
Sei sukh pailaam Raghav alaya.."

Raghav Pundit cooked food as preferred by Mahaprabhu himself and Mahaprabhu with his associates accepted the Prasad of Lord Radharaman with joy. Mahaprabhu was much pleased to find profound devotion in Raghav Pundit.

Thousands of people from different sides assembled at the place. Came Purander Pundit, Parameswar Pundit, Raghunath Vaidya, and also another Gadadhar known as Das Gadadhar, from nearer Ariadah, one of the beloved followers of lord Sri Chaitanyadev and thereafter associate of Nityananda. Here came Makardhwaj whom Mahaprabhu advised to look after Raghav Pundit so that he can bear the expenditure of service offered to devotees and followers from time to time. Mahaprabhu Sri Chaitanyadev expressed his sense of reality as shown in the house of Sri Baas at Kumarhatta. Mahaprabhu Sri Chaitanyadev here advised the Pundit to obey Nityananda as he obeys Him. Thus Mahaprabhu established Nityananda at Rghav Pundit's house at Panihati.

And from Raghav Pundit's house Nityananda's glory of spreding Harinaam to all categories of people of the society started. Panihati then got the importance like Nabadwip.

Barhanagar

After Panihati, Mahaprabhu Sri Chaitanyadev reached at Barhanagar, now called Baranagar, on the bank of the Ganga. Here He listened the citation of the Bhagabata read by the house owner and received immense joy. He sang and danced almost the whole of the night. Now the house is named Pathbari to all.

Coming back to Neelachal

After a few days roaming at Ramkeli, Shantipur,

Kumarhatta, Panihati, Baranagar and other places of devotees in Goud Bengal Mahaprabhu Sri Chaitanyadev returned at Neelachal the place of Lord Jagannath. Staring at Gadadhar said that for his attraction He could not proceed to Mathura and Vrindavan.

Gadadhar smilingly replied- Wherever you stay the place becomes Vrindavan. All the pilgrims including the Yamuna, the Ganga reach there to grace your presence.

At His return Pundit Gadadhar got much pleasure and at the same time felt sad as Mahaprabhu Sri Chaitanyadev could not travel in Mathura-Vrindavan despite He had an intention. He consoled Mahaprabhu it is true that for teaching others in the Country He is to travel but the rainy soason is about to start within a few days. In rainy season the roads become full of water, rivers become furiously over flooded. So, it is better to perform a journey after the rains. During this four months gap Mahaprabhu can maintain Chaturmasya.

All the followers who were present there admitted Pundit Gadadhar's advice to Lord Chaitanyadev and He could not rule out the suggestion given by Gadadhar. On hearing the news that Lord Chaitanyadev would stay in Puri for next four months all the people at Puri and the King Prataprudra got excitement in joy.

Mahaprabhu at Gadadhar's Place

Gadadhar invited Mahaprabhu Sri Chaitanyadev to

receive Prasd of Tota Gopinath, The Deity of Lord Sri Krishna. Mahaprabhu accepted the invitation with all of His other associates present in Neelachal.

Krishnadas Kabiraj illustrated the picture as:-

"Vikshaatey Punditera Sneha Prabhur Aaswadan
Maanusher Shaktye Dui Naa Hoi Barnan."

The holy situation of Gadadhar's love and respect to Lord Chaitanyadev and His tasting Prasad both cannot be explained in full by a mortal man on this universe.

13

MAHAPRABHU SRI CHAITANYADEV TO MATHURA-VRINDAVAN

According to Krishnadas Kabiraj

According to Krishnadas Kabiraj in *Sri Sri Chaitanya-charitamrita* Mahaprabhu Sri Chaitanyadev traveled in Mathura-Vrindavan only taking Balbhadra Bhattacharya and one of his Brahmin servant for necessary cooking. Through the dense forests of Jharikhanda Mahaprabhu reached Kasidham i.e. Varanasi and there He met Kashi Mishra as He promised earlier when He traveled in East Bengal. There with him He visited the Temples of Vishweshwar Shiva and Bindu Madhab. He met Chandrasekhar.

Prayag

From there Mahaprabhu Chaitanyadev went to Prayag the holy pilgrim of three river (The Ganga, the Yamuna and under currently flowing the Saraswati) junction i.e. Triveni Sangam. He took His bath in the holy water and was acquired by the feeling of Lord Sri Krishna as one of the rivers was Yamuna. He tries to jump into the water in love for Lord Sri Krishna but Balbhadra caught Him.

Mathura-Vrindavan

Then He moved towards Mathura and reached at Bishranti Ghat. From there Mahaprabhu Sri Chaitanyadev acquired with emotion of Lord Sri Krishna and bowed with folded hands for the birth place of Lord Sri Krishna. The place became full of Samkirtan led by Mahaprabhu Sri Krishna Chaitanyadev of expressing the glory of 'Krishnastu-bhagawanswayam' Lord Sri Krishna. There He met one disciple of Madhabendra Puri. Mahaprabhu's first preceptor is Ishwarpuri who is also disciple of Madhabendrapuri. Therefore, Mahaprabhu considered the person as of same shelf of Mahaprabhu's first preceptor Ishwarpuri and showed due respect. The person took Mahaprabhu to many Temples in Mathura-Vrindavan.

Mahaprabhu became confounded with the scene of forests, the trees and their leaves and creepers, the peacocks, the birds on the trees, especially Suk and Sari who always gossip on Lord Sri Krishna, the calves roaming around the cows. He sang and danced for Lord Sri Krishna. Then went to Madhutal, Kumud, Bahula and somewhere He embraced the deers in the forests. Once Mahaprabhu fell on thorn full bushes in tremendous excitement of passion for Lord Sri Krishna and remained unconscious. His accompanying person took Him to residence.

He went towards Arti village and discovered a paddy land as Radha Kunda where He sang and danced and bathed in the meager water of the land. The spectators were surprised to see His discovering and they joined and sang with Him in love for the entwind in bliss Radhakrishna.

Vrindavan and Other Places

Then He reached the Gobardhan hill where Lord Sri Krishna played His Lila. Then went to Suman Sagar and thereafter He remained at Akrur pilgrim by crossing the river Yamuna, seeing Bhadraban, Louhaban and other places of Lila Kshetra of Lord Sri Krishna-Radhakrishna. Then He reached Vrindaban, bathed at Kali lake where Kaliya was daunted by Lord Sri Krishna. He visited the place, the eternal RASHA sthal where Radhakrishna with other confidantes, played the eternal Rasha Lila. Sri Chaitanyadev became almost mad to visit the place. He sang and danced and He fainted in love of Lord Sri Krishna-Radhakrishna and gets conscience and again loses sense. Thousands of men come and feel fortunate by having a look of Mahaprabhu Sri Krishna Chaitanyadev. Another Krishnadas of Rajputana a devotee of Lord Sri Krishna-Radhakrishna came and started staying with and serve Sri Chaitanyadev.

A rumor rapidly spread that Lord Sri Krishna Himself is seen in Mathura-Vrindaban area for a few days and thousands of people from different corners were coming to Kaliya lake where as they heard Lord Sri Krishna was dancing on the great snake Kaliya daily but fail to find

---

**By Shri Radhakrishna Goswami (Radhu Goswami)*

Him. On hearing this rumor Balabhadra Bhattacharya sought permission from Sri Chaitanyadev to go to the spot and find dancing God but Sri Chaitanyadev replied - Being a knowledgeable man you should not talk like a fool. Yet, if you have strong desire, you can go not today but try tomorrow.'

Meanwhile, Sri Chaitanyadev collected the information what the real matter is. He came to know that recently at every night one fisherman catches fish in the water of the old Kaliya lake on a small boat fixing a little lamp hanging high. With the movement of the water the boat moves up and down and it causes the small lamp swing. Spectators from far see the twinkling light as a piece of gem is swinging as Lord Sri Krishna is dancing on the head of a big snake Kaliya to control it. Sri Chaitanyadev realized the truth and accordingly informed Balabhadra. This truth of illusion and the presence of Mahaprabhu in Mathura and Vrindavan both were so mixed that there Lord Sri Krishna was physically present rumor got its own wing.

Mahaprabhu although many a time earlier announced 'Mui Sei' as in confounded state for Lord Sri Krishna 'I am He' but now He advised not to consider any human being as God. A living being and God is not same. Living being is nothing but a smallest particle of the most burning and illuminating thing that remains for ever in the cosmic universe. It is true that God is in everybody but God does not flourish in same degree and same way in everybody.

We can understand that Mahaprabhu Sri Krishna Chaitanyadev forbidden us to consider a human being as God and He did not support any magic. Still to millions of followers He remained as God Himself. Devotees and followers do not want to be confused with any logic.

Return to Prayag

To avoid daily increasing crowd around Mahaprabhu, He decided to return to Prayag. On the way to return some cavalrymen pathan noticed Mahaprabhu lying unconscious under a tree and His followers were around Him. They thought that the followers have made the person mad or unconscious in order to rob the wealth of the ascetic person. They were carrying weapons and they thought it would be better if they themselves can rob the ascetic and the unarmed persons. But their evil purpose could not be successful as the Rajput devotee was brave enough to stop them from doing anything wrong by saying that he was well connected with Badshah and Badshahi soldiers would take care of any incident. It is better to wait till Mahaprabhu gets normal senses and verify the truth. After a while Mahaprabhu got normal senses. One of the Pathans was like a saint in gang asked some questions about religion to which Mahaprabhu not only answered but made the saint posing person His follower.

Krishnadas Kabiraj and Vrindavandas

Vrindavan Das has written *Sri Chaitanya Bhagabata* being inspired by his preceptor Nityananda Prabhu. He collected information from Nityananda Prabhu and other followers who used to travel Puri to meet Him. His writing was first named as Chaitanya Mangal but later the scholars of Vaishnavism considered the manuscript as compared as the *Srimad Bhagabata,* they proposed the name as *Sri Chaitanya Bhagawata.* This is some older than that of Krishnadas Kabiraj who in turn confessed many a time in the writing of Sri Sri Chaitanya-charitamrita, one of these is : -

"Bistari Barniaachhen Taahaa Das Vrindavan
Chaitanyalilaar Vyas Vrindavan Das

Madhur Kariya Lila Kariya Prakash..." A poet showed proper respect, love and modesty to another poet now a days is a rare incidence.

Tour at Mathura-Vrindavan

(according to Sri Chaitanya Bhagawat by Vrindavandas)

After remaining twelve years at a stretch in Puri Sri Chaitanyadev decided to go to Vrindavan Mathura through Bengal. By passing Atharonala, Cuttack reached in Ananta Mishra's house at Kulingram in Rarh area and He made the house full of Samkirtan whole day. He left there His cotton and hand knitted bed sheet, Kantha. It is learnt that in His memory there the Kantha was kept generations to generations.

Then Sri Chaitanyadev moved to Kumarhatta at Sri Baas's house. The house became full of Samkirtan with thousands of followers and devotees.

Shantipur

In Shantipur at Adwyaitacharya's house He met mother Sachidevi for the last time. He requested Adwyaitacharya and Sri Baas to look after mother Sachidevi.

Then He came to Khardah. He liked the people and the place and advised Nityananda Prabhu to settle there by marrying Basudha and Janhaba (Sri Ch. Bh. Antya, Chap. 11) :—

"Raha Adhikari Hoi Taraha Jagatey
Ichcha ye Kariba Bibha-Milibo Paschatey
Basudha Janhaba Naamey Lakshmi Saraswati."

Thus Nityananda Prabhu got the responsibility of being a family person by marrying Basudha and Janhaba daughters of Suryadas Sarkhel. Earlier Sri Chaitanyadev advised Nityananda Prabhu instead of meeting Mahapranhu in Puri at regular intervals he should take the charge to continue the publicity the name of God Sri Krishna among all people irrespective of castes and religions throughout Bengal.

Katwa

Then He arrived at Katwa and the people of Katwa got satisfaction to see Gadadhar Pundit with Sri Chaitanyadev as only Gadadhar Pundit can take proper care of Mahaprabhu and Mahaprabhu likes the company most. Sri Chaitanyadev found there Radhanath, a good chanter and well known singer. He asked him to chant some songs for Sri Krishna. Radhanath had no team and instruments with him then, but Sri Chaitanyadev aspired it and magically the place became full of sounds of all types of musical instruments and Radhanath started to sing. Thus Sri Chaitanyadev aroused the thousands of people gathered there with chanting Samkirtan.

"Sabey Gadadhar Prabhur Samhati Rahila, Suniya Katowar Lok Harashit Haila."

After taking bath there reached Roop and Sanatan and Mahaprabhu with Gadadhar, Roop and Sanatan started for Vrindavan.

On their way they visited many forests, rivers, villages, towns and became joyful by feeling the presence of God Sri Krishna with Sri Radha in everything and everywhere. Sri Chaitanyadev and Sri Gadadhar discussed about some secret things of Lord Radhakrishna and both of them became unconscious for some time repeatedly.

According to Vrindavan Das's writing Sri Chaitanyadev and Sri Gadadhar Pundit with Roop and Sanatan stayed in Vridavan-Mathura for about five years and visited all the Temples including 84 crosh (1.6 kms make 1mile, 2 miles make a crosh) Parikrama (encircling) on foot. Sri Chaitanyadev advised Roop and Sanatan to stay in Vridavan for reviving almost vanished abandoned Temples and Deities once left uncared in the jungles and to direct all the Vaishnavas by establishing and writing the Scriptures on various aspects. However, Vrindavan Das's writings do not tell much the details of their stay in vrindavan-mathura.

KRISHNADAS KABIRAJ'S DUE RESPECT TO VRINDAVANDAS

Vridavan-Mathura

Krishnadas Kabiraj offered due respect many a time to his predecessor Vrindavan Das's writing and so he has shortened some of the events to avoid repeatations. He has enlarged and expressed elaborately some of the tattwas (theories) and events that happened in the holy life of Lord Sri Chaitanyadev. From Kaviraj Goswami's writing, we find that Sri Chaitanyadev with Balbhadra Bhattacharya, again arrived in Varanasi after His tour in Vridavan-Mathura and stayed on the junction of the Ganga, the Yamuna and the Saraswati rivers at Tribeni. There Sri Roop with his younger brother Sri Ballav whose earlier name was Anupam Mullick stayed and were offered imense of His thoughts.

Sri Chaitanyadev tought Sri Sanatan, Sri Roop and Anupam

Mahaprabhu Sri Chaitanyadev tought for a period of two months all the essential and secret theories and even the theory 'Sadhya Sadhan Tattwa' that was established during the historic conversation with Roy Ramananda on His way towards Southern part of India.

Many people from different sides came to meet Him. Among them were a Brahmin of Maharashtra, Ballav Bhatta of Aulia Village and at last Sri Roop and Sri Ballav started journey for Vridavan-Mathura. There reached Sanatan Prabhu. Mahaprabhu Sri Chaitanyadev personally educated Sanatan Prabhu so that he with his brothers and others can preach properly millions of people of the world the theories of Sri Chaitanyadev and Vaishnavism specially the Goudiya Vaishnav thoughts. Sri Chaitanyadev advised him to join with his brothers in Vridavan-Mathura and to frame the theories of Vaishnavism with others who were sent by Him earlier. He also advised them to find the demolished and destroyed Temples in and around Vridavan-Mathura. He also advised them to look after all the people and devotees living below the poverty line and the lepors also.

Sri Chaitanyadev met Chandrasekhar and Tapan Mishra in Varanasi. Tapan Mishra being advised by Mahaprabhu in East Bengal stayed in Varanasi and Mahaprabhu for sometime stayed at his house according to His promise. There in the yard of Chandrasekhar's house when Mahaprabhu Sri Chaitanyadev was chanting with others—

"Hari Haraye Namah Krishna Jadabaya Namah,
Gopala Govinda Rama Sri Madhusudana."

There came eminent professor of Vedanta Prakashananda who once did not want to give due respect to Mahaprabhu Sri Chaitanyadev now expressed regret and bowed to Him by offering lot of respect.

Subuddhi Roy

Mahaprabhu Sri Chaitanyadev advised Subuddhi Roy to go to Vridavan-Mathura and chant the Lord Sri Krishna's name and work for the service for devotees who would reach there. Subuddhi Roy participated social work and religious work with Sanatan and others in Vridavan-Mathura.

At Narendra return of Sri Chaitanyadev in Neelachal

Sri Chaitanyadev decided to return Neelachal via Jharikhand. In the month of Baishakh (April-May) of 1437 Saka (1515 A.D.) Sri Chaitanyadev reached eighteen nallahs (Atharo Nala) and sent Balabhadra to Puri to give the information of His return to other followers and company. Near the Narendra Sarobar all from Puri came and met Him. Sri Chaitanyadev offered due respect and embraced each and everyone of His blessed and beloved. There assembled Paramanda Puri, Swarup Damodar, Pundit Gadadhar, Jagadananda, Gobinda, Bakreswar, Kashi Mishra, Pradyumna Mishra, Pundit Damodar, Haridas Thakur, Pundit Shankar and many others. Wherever Mahaprabhu goes the place becomes full of chanting the name of Sri Krishna by making the environment with celestial happiness.

14

RAJA PRATAP RUDRA MET SRI CHAITANYADEV

The His Highness King of Kalinga-Utkal Raja Pratap Rudra aspired to meet Sri Chaitanyadev but no one could make Him agreeable. The followers advised the King Pratap Rudra to see Him while He would be completely emerged in the emotion for God. One day Mahaprabhu Sri Chaitanyadev was fully engaged in chanting and dancing being encircled with other devotees the King saw Him and with utter surprise he noted that His chest is drenched with tears in love for Lord Sri Krishna. Raja Pratap Rudra became overwhelmed and the desire to meet Mahaprabhu Sri Chaitanyadev enhanced. The followers then arranged for teen aged son of the King to meet Mahaprabhu.

Mahaprabhu Sri Chaitanyadev was pleased to see the boy and blessed him. Then the followers during Angaraag session of Lord Gagannath, Balaram and Subhadra arranged a meeting of the King of Utkal with Mahaprabhu Sri Chaitanyadev in the garden of Mahaprabhu's residence at Kashi Mishra's house. To observe the signs of devotion in the King Mahaprabhu said,—I'm here for Ramananda Roy, Sarbabhoum and you the King. He embraced and blessed the Raja Pratap Rudra. Mahaprabhu in Vaishnavism made a bridge between people of high altitude and people of below the poverty line. In later days highly educated personalities like Sanatan-Roop-Jib-Adwyait-Gadadhar-Jagadananda and Basudev Mishra-Kashi Mishra-Roy Ramananda-Paramananda all followers admitted the aids and cooperation of the King.

Gadadhar Reads the Bhagwata

Gadadhar Pundit was engaged in worshipping of Tota Gopinath alone in Neelachal. Only for Mahaprabhu Sri Chaitanyadev he accepted the Mahaprabhu's advice to stay in Neelachal and worshipping of Tota Gopinath lonely. The unmarried, nice looking, modest with sweet voice and amiable nature devotee who does know nothing but Lord Sri Krishna and lifetime friend Sri Gouranga-Mahaprabhu-Sri Chaitanyadev. In every evening either Gadadhar Pundit goes to Mahaprabhu or He goes to Gadadhar because Sri Gadadhar reads with melodious voice the SrimadBhagabat daily and by listening to the reading Mahaprabhu Sri Chaitanyadev gets emotion and enjoyment as He liked this very much. They both with Swarup Damodar and other followers sing and dance in the name of Lord Sri Krishna. It was their regular programme.

"Gadadhar sanmukhe paren Bhagawat,
Shuniya prakashe Prabhu prembhav jato.

......

Bhagawat pathey Gadadhar mahasaya,
Damodar, Swaruper Kirtan bishaya."

Correction of Initiation Mantra of Gadadhar

One day Gadadhar requested Sri Chaitanyadev to make correction of the Initiation Mantra received from Pundarik Vidyanudhi in Nabadwip as somehow one or two letters from the Mantra is missing due to short of memories. The Initiation Mantras should be in tact, not a single letter should be dropped. Mahaprabhu replied - Do not be worried, Vidyanidhi is coming here within ten days."

Actually Pundarik Vidyanidhi arrived there and Gadadhar became surprised to see the assurance of Mahaprabhu has become fruitful and became joyful that the Initiation Mantra would be corrected by the preceptor. Mahaprabhu Sri Chaitanyadev and Pundarik Vidyanidhi both embraced each other happily and chanted the name of Lord Sri Krishna and danced in love for Lord Sri Krishna.

Vrindavandas wrote-

"Sribhakta batsal Gourchandra Narayan,
Premnidhi bakshey kari karen krandan."

After making necessary correction of the Mantra Vidyanidhi stayed in Neelachal with Swarup Damodar.

Krishnadas Kabiraj also wrote-

"Vidyanidhi se batsar Neeladri rahila,
Swarup sahit taar hoi sakhya-priti.
Duijanaar Krishna katha ekatrai sthiti,
Gadadhar pundite tinho punah Mantra dilaa."

Nityanandaprabhu and Raghava's Jhali

Mahaprabhu once advised Nityanandaprabhu not to come Neelachal on every occasion but to take the responsibility to preach millions of people of Goud Bengal in the name of Lord Sri Krishna. Nityanandaprabhu engaged himself in the work as per Mahaprabhu's advice. However, he could not resist himself of having a darshan of Lord Sri Chaitanyadev. And so, with the team of Adwyatacharya Sibananda Sen, Raghav Pundit, Makardhwaj Pundit and the members of the families of devotees from Goud Bengal he reached Neelachal. There were three persons carrying the Ragava's Jhali from Panihati (Sodepur).

Raghav's Jhali was prepared with all types of dried delicious food, pickles, sauce, sweet drops, various fries, etc. various kind of dry food as preferred by Sri Chaitanyadev for a year arranged by Raghava's sister Damayantidevi. Understanding that Sri Nityananda is coming to Neelachal Sri Chaitanyadev alone came forward to Kamalpur and received him cordially. There He met older Sri Adwyaitacharya also.

Sri Nityananda and Sri Gadadhar Pundit

Sri Nityananda arrived Neelachal with Raghav's Jhali. After handing over the Jhali to the associates of Sri Chaitanyadev like Govinda, Jagadananda, Swarup Damodar and others and having met Lord Sri

Chaitanyadev at Kamalpur ran towards the Temple of Lord Jagannath Prabhu.

Thereafter Sri Nityananda ran to Sri Gadadhar Pundit at Tota Gopinath. They had unthinkable attraction for each other. Their attraction to each other cannot be measured by men but by God Himself. The most polite and disciplined Sri Gadadhar Pundit always remains in deep thought of God Lord Sri Krishna and Lord Sri Chaitanyadev in heart and does the worship of Lord Gopinath Deity.

Vrindavandas described in Sri Chaitanyabhagwat (1st Division 2nd Chapter)—

"Jai Jai Prabhu Sri Gourasundara,
Jai Nityananda Gadadharer Jiban"

Again, Vrindavandas (Central Part 1st Chapter) bowed his head bty saying Sri Chaitanyadev is the 'Premdham of Sri Gadadhar and Sri Adwyait Prabhu.

He also described (Central Div. 3rd Chap.) Sri Chaitanyadev as Lord of Nityananda and Gadadhar.

Prabhu Nityananda reached the place at Temple of Gopinath where Gadadhar is busy with the materials for worshipping of Tota Gopinath with immense absorption in ecstasy. Gadadhar finds Sri Nityananda at the door. Both embraced with chests each other for a long time and cried for God. Tears flew unendingly. Both offered due respect to each other. Vrindavandas wrote this occasion—

"Bahjyagnan naahi dui Prabhur sareerey,
Dui Prabhu bhaasey bhakti ananda saagarey."

Sri Nityananda brought with him one mund (quintal) of fine rice and colored dress for Lord Gopinath. Gadadhar Pundit cooked the rice and thereafter offered the food to Lord Gopinath Deity. After worshipping, they were just ready to take Prasad and then heard from the door the call of Lord Sri Chaitanyadev-

"Gadadhar, Gadadhar, daakey Gourchandra,
Sambhramete Gadadhar bandye Padadawnda."

Sri Chaitanyadev laughingly said-l, I am not separated soul from you the two. If necessary, I shall establish my rights by force to have the Prasad.'

"Nityananda drabya Gopinather Prasad,
Tomaar randhan eethe aachhe mor bhag."

It is a great fortune for them that Himself Lord Sri Chaitanyadev has appeared at the place. Sri Nityananda and Sri Gadadhar Pundit was overwhelmed to get Lord Sri Chaitanyadev with them, they took Prasad along. The cooking was so delicious that Mahaprabhu praised Sri Gadadhar Pundit as he cooked in his earlier appearance as Radha in Baikunthadham.

"Bujhilam Baikunthey ranna karo tumi,
Tabe aar apanakey lukao ba keni."

Again, Vrindavandas wrote-

"Gadadhar subhadrishti karen jahare,
Se jaanite pare Nityananda swarupere.

Nityananda swarupe jaahaar priti money,
Lowaen Gadadhar jaanen sei joney.
Henamate Nityananda Prabhu Neelachaley,
Biharen Gourchandra saungey kutuhaley.
Tinjan ekatra thaken nirantar,
Srikrishna Chaitanya-Nityananda-Gadadhar. "

Dog too Eats Vegetables

Sibananda Sen makes necessary arrangements for those people who come from Goud Bengal and wants to stay for some days in Neelachal for Mahaprabhu and Sri Jagannath Prabhu in the Temple. Once he wanted to bring an ordinary pet dog with him. But the sailor of the boat of a river raised objection to take the dog on the boat. At last in lieu of ten Kadi the sailor agreed to take the dog on the boat. For a few days it disappeared and again it came to Mahaprabhu and started to remain with Him. Mahaprabhu showed His affection to it. Whatever residual vegetables Mahaprabhu threw to it the dog ate, even a half piece of hard coconut delightedly.

Sri Roop in Neelachal

Sri Roop Goswami came to see Lord Sri Chaitanyadev. Before coming he already started to write a drama on Lord Sri Krishna. On his way to Neelachal he had to stay at Satyabhamapur near Sakshi Gopal in Orissa. At night he saw in a dream that beautifully dressed and wearing precious ornaments a divine lady is directing him to write the drama on Lord Sri Krishna separately putting the character of the divine lady and that would bring a grand success. The Lady was Satyabhama, the another wife of Sri Krishna, he understood.

Mahaprabhu Lord Sri Chaitanyadev used to come to the hut of Haridas daily on His way from the Temple to residence and meet Haridas. Roop living with Haridas nearer to the residence of Mahaprabhu informed Him this fact. Mahaprabhu and Roy Ramananda were pleased to hear it and praised highly the beginning part of the Drama. Roop informed Mahaprabhu that Anupam has breathed his last in Goud Bengal.

Sanatan reached Neelachal

After ten days Sanatan reached in Neelachal by road and he also informed Mahaprabhu the premature demise of Anupam who was Mahaprabhu's one of the most affectionate youngster and a devotee of Lord Sri Ramchandra. Mahaprabhu Lord Sri Chaitanyadev advanced towards Sanatan to embrace but he went to far corner saying that during his way he was affected with the disease of skin so he did not want to touch Lord Sri Chaitanyadev. Mahaprabhu did not listen to his objection, He forcefully embraced him and made him introduced with all other associates who were present in Neelachal for the forthcoming annual Rathayatra of Jagannathprabhu. Sanatan also stayed with Haridas.

15

BALLAV BHATTA REACHED NEELACHAL

Once Mahaprabhu during His stay at Triveni-Prayag-Varanasi met Ballav Bhatta a Brahmin scholar in Vedanta of Aulia (Arail) village near Prayag and blessed him. At his house, Mahaprabhu was overwhelmed to listen the Sri Krishna Lila written by Raghupati Upadhyay. The whole village was resounded with chanting of songs of Lord Sri Krishna by Sri Chaitanyadev and the thousands of people gathered there.

That Ballav Bhatta came to Neelachal to meet Mahaprabhu. Mahaprabhu introduced him with other followers. He read some slokas on Mahaprabhu and then started to read the explanation of Srimad Bhagawat written by himself to Mahaprabhu. After listening to a few lines of his explanation Mahaprabhu stopped him saying - I do not want to listen to other than writings on Srimad Bhagawat as explained by Sridhar Swami.'

He rebuked him too. Being hurt by Mahaprabhu Ballav Bhatta wandered door to door to read his explanation but no one agreed to listen any explanation what Mahaprabhu does not recommend. Although Mahaprabhu rebuked him and He gave suggestion to worship Lord Sri Krishna sincerely and to work on the path of Sridhar Swami.

Sri Sundarananda Vidyavinode in his 'Achintyavedavedbaad' Ballavacharya was from a Brahmin of Andhra Pradesh. He was of Bhardwaj Gotra under Taittariya branch of the Yayurveda. He was born in Baisakh of 1479 in a forest named Champaranya near Raipur in Madhya Pradesh. His father Lakshman Bhatta with his pregnant wife was returning home fleeing from Kashidham (Varanasi) learning possible attack by the then rulers.

Afterwards Ballav Bhatta started his education in Varanasi and learnt Vaishnav Scriptures under Madhabananda Yoti there. In Vijayanangar near his maternal uncle's house, he met Srivyasthirtha at the court of King of Vijayanangar. Easily he could defeat 'Mayavaad' and established the 'Suddhadwitavaad'. Srivyasthirtha awarded him 'Acharya' title. It is learnt that he roamed throughout India thrice. Second time, at his thirty, he married and considering Kashi holy place of God Shiva Mahadeva would not suit for dwelling with family. He settled at Arail Village off Prayag. Here he brought Mahaprabhu Sri Chaitanyadev when Mahaprabhu stayed at Prayag-Varanasi and taught Sri Sanatan and Sri Roop there.

Dr. S. Radhakrishnan wrote in 'Indian Philosophy' Vol. 11, p. 756 - "He accepts the authority not only of Upanishadas, the Bhagavadagita and the Brahma-sutra; but also of the Bhagabat Puran. In his works Anubhasya, Siddhantarahasya and Bhagabattika Subodhini he offers theistic interpretation of Vedanta, which differs from those of Sankara and Ramanuja."

Gadadhar Pundit Eased Ballav Bhatta's Vanity

One day Jagadananda invited Mahaprabhu with His all associates present in Neelachal including Ballav Bhatta. There came Gadadhar Pundit so calmly and politely that to see Gadadhar Ballav Bhatta was overwhelmed. He thought this is the person for whom he was in search of. He was feeling that his attitude of boasting himself for the writing should be amended but he was not getting any chance to wipe it out. He saw the most modest Gadadhar Pundit to come to this invitation. He thought if he takes the shelter of Gadadhar Pundit he may ease his problem and he may think of Lord Sri Krishna by leaving his "Ism". Lord Sri Chaitanyadev's most beloved company since His childhood Gadadhar Pundit was sincerely fond of Srimad Bhagawat and could not say 'No' to anyone. Noticing Ballav Bhatta's eagerness agreed to listen the explanation of Srimad Bhagawat as written by Ballav Bhatta. But there remains one 'But' that without the approval of Mahaprabhu, Gadadhar Pundit cannot walk a single step. Lord Sri Chaitanyadev expressed jokingly false grief to His lifetime friend that Ballav Bhatta meets Gadadhar Pundit daily to read that Srimad Bhagawat and so Gadadhar Pundit felt embarrassed.

Again Ballav Bhatta meets Lord Sri Chaitanyadev and begged mercy for his audacity. After a few days, he invited Mahaprabhu with all the associates. After the grand festival of Kirtan and taking Prasad, he approached Lord Sri Chaitanyadev in presence of Gadadhar Pundit that he wants to be more corrected and purified by getting initiation from Gadadhar Pundit. He bowed his head to Sri Chaitanyadev and Gadadhar Pundit. Mahaprabhu seeing his eagerness to wipe out his vanity by getting shelter from His beloved Gadadhar Pundit approved it. Gadadhar Pundit initiated Ballav Bhatta with the esoteric words Gopal Mantra.

Then Ballav Bhatta set for Vrindavan to worship more sincerely and to participate in the big work of Lord Sri Chaitanyadev with Sri Sanatan, Sri Roop, Sri Jib (son of Anupam), Gopal Bhatta and others there engaged in reviving the lost Temples and establishing the Goudiya Vaishnav Scriptures.

In "Sri Ballavacharyajiki Nijabarta" published from Virbijoy Press at Ahmedabad and also in "Samprayaday Pradipey" published from Kankroli Vidyabhibhag we get the confirmation of Mahaprabhu's once presence at Aarail Viallage.

Kavi Karnapur has also confirmed that as the writer of Sobhodhini Explanation Ballavacharya and Ballav Bhatta is one and the same person.

Others who took Shelter in Gadadhar

In 12th Section of the Sri Sri Chaitanyacharitamrita Krishnadas Kabiraj described the branch of Gadadhar Pundit the best one. He has cited the names e.g. "Dhrubananda, Sridhar Brahmachari, Bhagawatacharya Haridas Brahmachari, Ananta Acharya, Kavi Dutta, Nayan Mishra, Gangamantri Mamuthakur, Bhugarva

Gossain, Bhagawat Das, Baninath Brahmachari, Ballav Chaitanyadas, Srinath Chakraborty, Uddhavdas, Jeeta Mishra, Wood cutter Jagannathdas, Srihari Acharya, Sadipuriya Gopal, Krishnadas Brahmachari, Pushpa Gopal, Sri Harsa, Raghu Mitra, Pundit Lakshminath, Bangabati Chaitanyadas, Sriraghunath, Sibananda Chakraborty, Amogh Pundit, Hasti Gopal, Chaitanya Ballav, Jadu Ganguly, Mongal Vaishnav" and we may cite the names of Ballv Bhatta, Lokenath Goswami, Jagadananda and Adwyaitachary's son Achyutananda whom Mahaprabhu took up in His arms just after His Sannyas. These all and others whom Mahaprabhu considered fit for becoming His associates to run the Vaishnav Movement throughout India sent to His lifelong partner and sevak Gadadhar Pundit for giving them initiation mantra.

Millions of Followers in Neelachal on the Rathayatra

On the occasion of the Rathyatra Festival millions of followers with the members of their families from whole Bengal, Assam, Tripura, Orissa and other parts of the Country started to come to Neelachal. Sri Adwyaitacharya led a big team. Before this Sri Nityananda Prabhu reached with Raghav's Jhali. Lord Sri Chaitanyadev advanced up to the Eighteen drains (Atharo nallah). With Lord Sri Chaitanyadev the followers of Puri, Gadadhar Pundit, Paramananda Puri and Nityananda the others like Roy Ramananda, Basudev Saarbabhoum, Jagadananda, Kashi Mishra, Adwyaitacharya's son

Achyutananda, Pundit Gadadhar's brother Baninath, Swarup Damodar. Pradyumna Mishra and others reached the Aathaaro Nallah.

The atmosphere of the place changed into Divinity with the songs and dances by the devotees and Mahaprabhu for the love for Lord Sri Krishna. All they including old Adwyaitacharya, modest Gadadhar and powerful Sri Nityananda played in the water of Narendra Sarobar with cheerful mood, cheerful because of God and the presence of Lord Sri Chaitanyadev who always remain in deep thoughts for God Lord Sri Krishna. Afterwards Mahaprabhu started to proceed towards the Temple of Jagannath with all the persons. One of the devotees remained ahead of Sri Chaitanyadev with a tub of Tulsi tree as Mahaprabhu said - like a fish without water I can hardly live without Tulsi. Tulsi was favourite of Lord Sri Krishna.'

Mahaprabhu Himself Washed the Temple Places

It is natural everyday millions of devotees from all over the Country come to the Temple to have darshan of Lord Jagannath and so the floors of the Temple and temple yard become full of dust. It is also true that every day some people engaged in cleaning also sweeps and washes. But it is not sufficient for a big festival. Mahaprabhu before the Chariot Festival started to wash the floors of Gundicha Temple and to see it other devotees and followers joined to cleanse the Temple.

16

THE GREATEST CHARIOT OF LORD JAGANNATH

The Yatra of the Greatest Chariot of Lord Jagannath, Lord Balaram and Their sister Subhadradevi. Despite the pulling by many strong and able bodied men the Chariots did not move. The King arranged all the elephants in possession. But they too failed. Mahaprabhu Sri Chaitanyadev called all people of all castes of Puri and all those assembled in the festival to pull the Chariots with chanting songs of God. Mahaprabhu Sri Chaitanyadev Himself pushed from backsid with His head and took part by dancing and singing for Lord Sri Krishna and the festival got an added attraction of His participation with the teams of thousands of people singing and dancing. At first the His Highness the King swept, as prevailing convention, the starting point of the path of Holy Chariots with golden broom and then the Holy Chariots from the Main Temple moved towards the Gundicha Temple. Mahaprabhu Sri Chaitanyadev danced and chanted the songs of God in front of the gala procession of the movement of the Chariots. The most fortunate people witnessed the beauty of the participation of the King, Mahaprabhu Sri Chaitanyadev and thousands of devotees from all over the Country singing and dancing around the nicely decorated Holy Chariots. (Surprisingly, Mahaprabh was found at seven places in the long procession at the same time and sometime at the front with singing and dancing in love for Jagannath Prabhu.)

Vaishnav Families in Neelachal

After the Rathayatra all the Vaishnava families who gathered in Neelachal wanted to cook for and feed Mahaprabhu Sri Chaitanyadev at their temporary residences there. All by cooking food as preferred by Sri Chaitanyadev they got complete satisfaction. But Sitadevi the wife of Adwyaitacharya wanted to cook for and feed to only Mahaprabhu Sri Chaitanyadev. The thing was not so easy because no one could get Him alone. Hundreds of followers always liked to accompany Him. As a practice Mahpprabhu advises to give all delicious food to others and to accept only ordinary vegetable curry called 'Lafra'. At last on the very day and at the time of His invitation at the residence of Adwyaitacharya as God desired a heavy storm broke out. No one could move a step. Sri Chaitanyadev found the storm not so much strong that He cannot move. So, alone Sri Chaitanyadev left His place to reach the residence of Sitadevi and Adwyaitacharya and found the house only is out of strong storm. The couple thus got full satisfaction by serving with all types of delicious food to Sri Chaitanyadev. Perhaps they had some important discussions that should not be discussed in presence of others.

Lakshapati (millionaires)

Sri Chaitanyadev cannot accept everybody's invitation daily as the number of aspirants to invite and feed Mahaprabhu was more than the days of their stay in Neelachal for the four months of Chaturmasya. Therefore, He announced He would accept invitation from Lakshapati (millionaires) only. All became stunned to learn that only a millionaire here could invite their beloved Sri Chaitanyadev whose most of the followers were mainly the people of below poverty line. Moreover, Sri Chaitanyadev did not indulge any kind of differences in respect of caste or financial ability or anything. The people fell in dilemma and by understanding it Mahaprabhu Sri Chaitanyadev made it clear that if a devotee takes daily one lakh number of name of Lord Sri Krishna, the 'Jap' Mantra, he would be termed as Lakshapati and be able to feed Prasad at his residence. The question of financial ability does not arise at all. He wanted to see all to utter the name of Lord Sri Krishna all along.

The Song for Lord Sri Chaitanyadev

On the other side, Sri Adwyaitacharya gave direction to Sri Baas and other followers to sing the song for Lord Sri Chaitanyadev. Sri Baas did the same but He wanted that all would sing for Lord Sri Krishna only.

"Bolo Krishna Bhajo Krishna Suno Krishna Naam,
Krishna Hau Sabaar Jiban Dhan Pran."

Or

"Bhajo Krishna, Kaho Krishna, Laho Krishner Naamre,
Je Jan Krishna Bhaje Se Hoi Aamaar Pranre."

Yet, the millions of devotees and the followers under the leadership of Nityananda prabhu and Sri Baas started to sing for Lord Sri Chaitanyadev—

"Bhajo Gouranga, Kaho Gouranga, Laho Gouranger Naamre,
Je Jan Gouranga Bhaje Se Hoi Aamaar Pranre. "

Despite His objection the song 'Bhajo Gouranga...' He could not resist the mass. So, He remains with bending the head and keeps Himself mum and thinks of Lord Sri Krishna in Himself.

Visit Jagannath Temple first

In the opinion of millions of followers and devotees Lord Sri Krishna Chaitanya is Himself Lord Sri Krishna. Brahmnanda once started to say that Sri Chaitanyadev is mobile Jagannath. Mahaprabnu cannot accept these compliments and so, He directed each and everyone to visit the Temple first then to come to Him. The same direction was also applicable for Sri Nityanandaprabhu, Roy Ramananda and all His closed associates.

Haridas Leaves the Earth on the Lap of Mahaprabhu

Haridas leaves the Earth. It is known to all that Haridas came to Puri and Mahaprabhu arranged a little room in the garden nearer to the residence of Mahaprabhu in the house of Kashi Misra. Haridas there used to cite Harinaam silently and sometime chanting the whole day and night. He tried to complete chanting and citing silently Harinaam three lakh times a day. Sometime it took much time so, he could not get time to have Prasad in the lunch daily arranged by Mahaprabhu. Mahaprabhu used to take Prasad after sending Prasad to Haridas by the hand of His all time associate Gobinda. One day hearing that Haridas is ill and cannot move or cannot take Prasad Mahaprabhu came to see him. Haridas was thin and lean and crying for he cannot complete three lakh time citing and chanting for Lord Sri Krishna. To see, Mahaprabhu Himself attended at the hut. Haridas said in low voice that he desires to leave this world before Mahaprabhu. He requested Him to please arrange it. The next day Lord Sri Chaitanyadev arrived in the hut and took him on His lap. Haridas and other blessed followers started to chant Harinaam and some time later he breathed his last lying on the Lap of Lord Sri Chaitanyadev. Mahaprabhu Himself carried him to the seashore and buried him there.

Then Lord Sri Chaitanyadev begged for Prasad to observe obsequies for Haridas. All the devotees including the Her Highness Queen sent lot of Prasad for the ritual. Mahaprabhu for some time remained silent to bear with the shock for one of the most pure and most beloved devotees Haridas's demise. Haridas was His own man and He considered him as His elder one in taking the name of Lord Sri Krishna from the very beginning. His shock was natural, after all Mahaprabhu appeared on this earth for love, love to all i.e. love to Sri Krishna.

in the [illegible] duly arranged by Mahaprabhu. Mahaprabhu used to [illegible] Prasad after [illegible] Prasad to Chandru by his hand of his [illegible]. One day hearing that [illegible] and came [illegible] Prasad. Mahaprabhu came to see him. Chandru was [illegible] and [illegible] crying for he cannot control [illegible] and [illegible] Lord [illegible] Mahaprabhu Himself [illegible] at the [illegible]. [illegible] to these strange [illegible] and [illegible]. Chandru [illegible] other [illegible] in the name of [illegible] [illegible]

17

AFFECTION OF MAHAPRABHU SRI CHAITANYADEV TO CHILDREN

Mahaprabhu Sri Chaitanyadev came across a good number of children and juniors during His time. The first was 'His Gadadhar' son of Madhab Mishra. Gadadhar was a loveable boy for his amiable and modest character and moreover he was a devotee of Lord Sri Krishna from the Childhood. Gadadhar Pundit liked to decorate Mahaprabhu with garlands of flowers and painting 'Tilak' of sandal wood pastes before starting the chanting and dancing for Lord Sri Krishna. Gadadhar remained all along Mahaprabhu in this world and their friendship continued for ever.

Bhakta Haridas known as Yaban Haridas always used to chant the name of Lord Sri Krishna. At his old age he used to take the Harinaam Mantra 3 (three) lakh times a day. He received whips on his body at twentytwo market places and thus was forced to leave Harinaam. But he did not leave Harinaam from his lips. He was associated with Adwyaitacharya and in time he joined the team of Harinaam led by Mahaprabhu Sri Chaitanyadev. Although he was an elderly devotee and follower for his simplicity in natural behaviour was like a child to Sri

Chaitanyadev. He received maximum adorn from Mahaprabhu. Mahaprabhu let him breath his last on His lap and cried for his demise and Himself also carried his body for burial under the sands at the seashore.

At Sri Baas Angan in Nabadwip when Mahaprabhu was engaged with chanting and dancing almost the whole day, one day He found a little girl of about four years' old crying for something. This little girl was known as Narayani, daughter of Sri Baas's deceased eldest brother Nalini. Her crying drew the attention of Lord Sri Gouranga. Mahaprabhu told her, **"why you are crying mum".**

He paused and advised - ***"If you want to cry, cry for Lord Sri Krishna, utter Sri Krishna."*** Surprisingly the four years' child started to cry by saying 'Haa Krishna, Krishna, Krishna Hey' and tears from her eyes started to fall. To see it Mahaprabhu was pleased and blessed her. Mahaprabhu gave her the end of food eaten up almost every day while she was in Nabadwip.

Later Narayani was married to one Brahmin person of Kumarhatta named Baikunthadas. Unfortunately that Baikuntha expired leaving her pregnant. Sri Baas brought this fatherless and husbandless carrying girl to his house at Kumarhatta. There on Krishnaa dwadashi (12th day of new moon) in 1429 Saka Narayani gave birth to a male baby. This baby afterwards became Vrindavandas, the Vyas of Sri Chaitanya episode.

The child Achyutananda son of Adwyaitacharya also received affection from Mahaprabhu many times and later he was initiated from Sri Gadadhar Pundit and became one of the important followers of Sri Chaitanyadev.

At His walking towards the west for Vrindavan-Mathura just after initiation from Keshab Bharati Mahaprabhu reached four crosh away from Bakreswar through the Rarh area but with the efforts of others who followed Him was to return. The season was the spring. The Rarh area was full of red Simul, Palash, etc. flowers with gentle breeze. But Mahaprabhu was fed up as He could not find anybody to utter the name Lord Sri Krishna. Once on the north bank of the river Ajoy there lived the Great Poet Jaydev, the writer of 'Gita Govindam'. Mahaprabhu told His intimates better to leave this earth and at that time a teen aged boy beyond the cattle in the nearer field shouted 'Haribol' and Mahaprabhu became charmed and patted the boy.

Sri Jib was son of Anupam the youngest brother of Sri Roop and Sri Sanatan. After premature death of Anupam Sri Jib got affection from Roop-Sanatan and also from Sri Chaitanyadev and could work for writing on Vaishnav Philosophy in due time.

At first Mahaprabhu was not agreeable to give permission to meet Him to His Highness the King of Utkal but He allowed his tender aged son and blessed him. Later the King Prataprudra got the favour of Lord Sri Chaitanyadev.

Once, Sibananda Sen arrived Neelachal with his family. To see Mahaprabhu his seven years' old son started to chew one old finger of His foot. Mahaprabhu repeatedly said to him to leave Him but the boy of seven did not reply Mahaprabhu understood. He would show him His real feature he might leave the foot for the time. At last, Lord Sri Chaitanyadev showed the pertinacious boy His appearance. The boy saw Him as Lord Sri Krishna and himself started to compose a poem and started to recite-

> *"Shrabasoh Kubalayamkshmoranjana Suraso Mahendramonidasah,*
> *Vrindavana Taruninang Mandalamakhilam Harirjoyati"....*

It means that, He who remains as ornaments on the ears, He who remains on the chests as the necklace with Nilkantha gem and pearls, He who remains as all types of ornaments of all the Universe on the whole body of the Brajanganas, let His grace be victorious.

Lord Sri Chaitanyadev was stunned to hear it from a boy of seven. The boy's talent is so poetic? It is sure that one day in future this boy would be a poet. So, Sri Chaitanyadev named him as Kavi Karnapur. Really, this Paramananda Sen Son of Sibananda Sen became a follower and renowned poet and writer in the Vaishnav Literature and Philosophy in Vrindavan.

We can easily say that Sri Chaitanya Mahaprabhu had immense love for children. He considered today's Children are the future of the Nation and the Mankind. Mahaprabhu Sri Chaitanyadev was God of Love. He loved God Sri Krishna and He loved all the human beings irrespective of castes, creeds, religions, nationality, colours, ages and whatever distinguishing factors people have.

Respect by Mahaprabhu to Sri Ram, Shiva Mahadeva and Shakti Devi (Sri Kali, Sri Durga and Others)

Gourangadev gave due respect to Sri Ram Chandra, Sri Devadidev Mahadev Shiva, the Mother goddess of Shakti, Sri Kali - Sri Durga and to all the gods and the goddesses and advised all. He did not see any difference in Sri Ram and Sri Krishna. During the journey in the South on foot almost alone through forests, rivers, hills, in the winter or in the rains He visited Temples of all the gods and the goddesses at every point with one song always in lips :-

Rama Raghava Rama Raghava Rama Raghava raksha maang
Krishna Keshaba Krishna Keshaba Krishna Keshaba paahi maang.

This song was enchanted also in Nabadwip Lila. He had love for monkeys likewise after a few years Tulsidas the greatest devotee and poet on Sri Ramchandra used to like monkey and himself shown immense respect for Bhakta Hanumanji. Gourangadev had a companion Murari who used to worship Ramchandraji. He also at later period in Puri thanked him for not leaving own God's feet.

At the time of demise of Jagannath Mishra the only remaining son Nemai like an ordinary son assuming that father is to breath his last asked him mourning - To whom you're leaving me behind going for ever?" He replied - at the feet of Raghunath, Sri Ramchandraji would protect you."

Once in Neelachal Mahaprabhu danced and jumped with others as the monkey soldiers of Sri Ramchandraji at a procession of Dashera festival i.e.Vijaya Dashami that regarded as the festival of victory of Sri Ramchandraji over Ravana.

He had also natural respect to the goddess Durga, Kali, the goddess of power. On the way to Shantipur with Nityananda, He met a devotee of mother Kali and accepted his hospitality by taking fruits as token. On the way to Puri at Bansdhai He met another anchorite and with wonderful patience and due respect talked and got information about others in the line. In the concluding act of the drama His one entry was in the dress of Adya Shakti the original goddess of power. Many of his followers recited slokas of goddess of power and they worshipped Him as the Mother on the stage.

He also was a great fan of Shiva. Once in Nabadwip a singer on Shiva came to their house and Mahaprabhu jumped on his shoulder crying, "Muin Shiva, Muin Shankar." His associate Mukunda recited Shiva-Mahimna stotra. He visited Jaleswar, Kapoteswar, Bhubaneswar Shivas. He took bath at Markendaya pilgrimage. He with heart showed His respect at Shivakanchi, Setubandha and many other Shiva Temples. He advised all to utter the name Lord Sri Krishna but to worship with own belief own God and the gods-goddesses first.

Mahaprabhu Hard Nut to Crack

Sri Krishnachaitanya Mahaprabhu although was an incarnation of love for all sometime becomes hard and merciless if discipline and dignity is overtaken by any of His beloved associates. He always taught all to offer due and proper dignity to all human beings, even to every creature. But He remained unbreakable when one of associates broke the discipline of a Vaishnav mendicant. Another Haridas called as young Haridas once fell into the prey of Mahaprabhu's hard cruelty. He was an excellent chanter of songs on Lord Sri Krishna and was favoured by Mahaprabhu. One day eminent scholar of Vedanta Gopal Acharya advised young Haridas to bring one mound of fine rice from Madhuri Devi, sister of Sikhi Mahiti in the name of Gopal Acharya because he desired to offer Prasad to Mahaprabhu and His associates. Young Haridas did so and brought that rice for Sri Chaitanyadev. At the time of taking Prasad Sri Krishnachaitanya Mahaprabhu found the rice is made of precious rice. He enquired from where the fine rice was available and came to know that it is Young Haridas who brought from Madhuridevi. Mahaprabhu considered Sikhi Mahiti, Swarup Damodar, Roy Ramananda and Madhuridevi as own people of Radhika of Vridavanlila. He became furious to Young Haridas and ordered the door to be closed for Young Haridas immediately. Thus, one of the beloved excellent singer of the Team of Samkirtan Choto Haridas was rejected forever by Mahaprabhu.

No one could convince Him to withdraw His order. Door was closed, closed for ever even for one of the most favourite associates. He was so hard. At last Young Haridas at Prayag left this earth.

Mahaprabhu did not listen to the notes written by Ballavacharya on Bhagawat as it defied the established and already accepted narration of Sridhar. At last, Mahaprabju advised him to ease his vanity by taking shelter under Gadadhar.

Not a Luxurious Life to Enjoy

One day Jagadananda, engaged in looking after the external affairs, took some fragrant substance from Sibananda Sen and prepared of sandalwood scented oil for Sri Chaitanyadev and gave it to Gobinda who used to look after the personal matters of Sri Chaitanyadev. Gobinda informed Him but He replied it would be better for lighting lamps of Jagannathprabhu. On another day Gobinda reminded Sri Chaitanyadev that the oil may help to keep head calm and it may also help sound sleep at night. Sri Chaitanyadev replied that He has not taken the life of a Sannyasi (medicant) for a luxurious life to enjoy. Jagadananda threw the pitch full of scented oil on the courtyard. Jagadananda at his room remained without taking any food for three days. Sri Chaitanyadev heard this, reached at his room, and requested him break the fasting, as He will receive Prasad at his place. That is His feeling for a hurt associate.

Once Mahaprabhu advised Raghunathdas Goswami and all to lead simple life i.e. not to consume rich and costly food and in much quantity and wear rich dresses.

'Bhalo naa khaibe, Bhalo naa Paribe.' Mahaprabhu preferred to get Prasad of simple rice and lafra (one type curry of mixed vegetables) and distributed the delicious Prasad to other followers accompanied Him.

Not to Cross One's Limit

One day Sanatan in Neelachal expressed his hesitation that he is affected with bad skin disease and so, he cannot mix every devotee. Jagadananda himself advised him to return to Vrindavan. Sri Krishnachaitanya Mahaprabhu learnt it and rebuked Jagadananda that he should not cross his limit by advising Sanatan whom He has given shelter.

With Mahaprabhu's touch Sanatan was cured of disease and stayed in Neelachal for more ten months having discussions with Sri Krishnachaitanya Mahaprabhu on Vaishnav Philosophy.

Not to give Pain to Others

Mahaprabhu advised all not to give pain to any creation. All are God's creations.

"Kayamonobakyey Pranimaatre na dibe udbeg"

Mahaprabhu did not spare Sachimaa as she felt some anger in mind towards Adwyaitacharya as once gave his company of wisdom to build up her son Vishwarup. That

Vishwarup went out taking Sannyas. When Gourangadev was becoming ready for this world the same Adwyaitacharya started to give his company. Mother Sachidevi so was afraid of the 52 years' elder Adwyaitacharya lest her only remaining son Nemai may leave the house for taking Sannyas. Due to Sachimaa's suspicion Adwyaitacharya perhaps got pain. This is also one kind of Vaishnav Aparadha. Afterwards, on Nemai's request Sachimaa sought apology from Adwyaitacharya and relieved from Vaishnav Aparadha.

Hard Reality and Sri Chaitanyadev

Mahaprabhu Sri Chaitanyadev naturally had thoughts for hard reality. Once at the house of Sri Baas at Kumarhatta Mahaprabhu found that Sri Baas is running family in acute hardship because he never begged for himself. Mahaprabhu advised Ramai Pundit and other brothers including some devotees to look after this aspect so that Sri Baas can maintain the family easily and then he would be able to think of Lord Sri Krishna.

Once in Nabadwip Mahaprabhu during the songs and dances called ordinary retailer of banana cones at corner of market Sridhar from whom He used to take banana cones gave him due respect in His team of Samkirtan.

He also blessed Suklambar Brahmachari an ordinary beggar by eating a handful of begged mixed rice from his bag and included him in His team of Samkirtan.

Mukunda, a friend of Gadadhar Pundit, is a devotee and composes songs on various topic on Lord Sri Krishna and sings, is also an expert Physician. Mahaprabhu advised him to continue the profession of a Physician for his earning and for the benefit of persons fallen in illness.

Basudev Dutta a well to do devotee spends money extravagantly. Mahaprabhu advised another well to do devotee Sibananda Sen, who arranges to bring devotees and followers and their residences at Puri every year to see the matter so that Basudev cannot spend much extravagantly in each occasion. He wanted all to think where to spend and how much to afford.

Banamali Pundit came to Sri Chaitanyadev to beg. He blessed the father and son and they got so much benefit that they have been blessed by God Himself.

Mahaprabhu Sri Chaitanyadev several times took the work to clean the temples at Neelachal and during His Nabadwip Lila also thinking the health aspects of thousands of devotees who gather at the sites.

Once Mahaprabhu Sri Chaitanyadev advised Sri Sanatan and also Subuddhi Roy to look after the followers and devotees who will reach Mathura-Vrindavan.

Mahaprabhu occasionally used to arrange to send clothes and Prasad for Sachidevi at Nabadwip and used to tell some of the followers to look after Mother Sachidevi in His absence.

To Give Due Respect to Women

Mahaprabhu Sri Chaitanyadev knew very well that without women this world cannot run. They are as equal as Men. There should not remain any differences in Men and Women. So, He advised not to hurt any woman but to keep respectable distances with women other than mother, sister, wife, daughter and closed kith and kins. The women generally become more devout than men.

They are highly respectable. Every man cannot control him and so there remains chances of fall and the society becomes dirty. A Vaishnab is worshipper of God Lord Sri Krishna so he needs to remain pure in every respect. For a Vaishnav there are some rules that should be maintained by each and every devotee. Younger Haridas perhaps had crossed the boundary and so for him Mahaprabhu closed the door forever, Mahaprabhu always used to bow to devout women of any category.

He is once said—

Even a prostitute with devotion for Lord Sri Krishna should get due respect from Society.

**By Shri Radhakrishna Goswami (Radhu Goswami)*

18

EIGHTEEN YEARS AT NEELACHAL

During 1486 A.D. to 1533 A.D. in almost forty eight years Mahaprabhu remained in Nabadwip for 24 years, out of another 24 years He used 6 years in traveling in Southern India, Vrindavan-Mathura and Shantipur-Katwa-Panihati and some places in Bengal. During the next 18 years of His stay in Neelachal only for 6 years Mahaprabhu was in touch with all His beloved and blessed by teaching every necessary thing for becoming a pure Vaishnav.

During the last 12 years mahaprabhu remained almost silent and was absorbed in the thoughts of Radhakrishna's eternal divine lila.

RADHAKRISHNA

Once for ten days Mahaprabhu Sri Chaitanyadev trained Sri Roop Goswami at the Dashaswamedh Ghat in Varanasi. Thereafter in Varanasi known as Kashi the place of Lord Shiva Mahadeva Mahaprabhu trained Sri Sanatan Goswami for long two months the necessity of Love for God, Lord Sri Krishna. Sanatan in his earlier family life was also a scholar and he used to manage the post of Prime Minister in the court of King Hussain Shah.

During their stay in Vrindavan-Mathura except doing the job of revival of lost Temples and Dieties Sri Roop and Sri Sanatan wrote lot of Vaishnav Scriptures.

Sri Roop wrote dramas like Bidagdha Madhava, Lalit Madhava, on analytical rhetoric and poetics like Ujjalnilmoni, Rasamrita Sindhu, Padyavali (collection of poems, rhymes) etc.

Sri Sanatan Goswami wrote Brihadbhagawatamritam, Brihadvaishnavtoshini and also took part in writing the rites and rules of Vaishnavism the Haribhaktivilasa.

All these things Mahaprabhu talked and discussed with the closed associates Swarup Damodar, Roy Ramananda, Sarbabhoum, Jagadananda and others few in Neelachal during this period.

However, for the 12 years Mahaprabhu could speak little. He did not feel necessary to move from Neelachal and remained in Himself in GAMBHIRA at Kashi Mishra's house. Mahaprabhu Sri Chaitanyadev used to meet Gadadhar Pundit at Tota Gopinath Temple with thirst to listen to Bhagawat read by Gadadhar almost every afternoon. Thereafter He used to return to GAMBHIRA resting hands on the shoulders of Swarup Damodar or Govinda or Jagadananda or Roy Ramananda or on Gadadhar.

In this period Jagadananda, a disciple of Sri Gadadhar Pundit and engaged for service with Mahaprabhu went to Nabadwip to see Sachimaa. This was for annual communication on behalf of Mahaprabhu. He took clothes for her and Prasad of Jagannath Prabhu perhaps for Vishnupriyadevi and other devotees, followers at Nabadwip. After one month he returned to Neelachal with a message written by Adwyaitacharya and handed it over to Sri Chaitanyadev. The meaning of the letter was incomprehensible for any other person. Sri Chaitanyadev read the letter and smiled for a while.

Mahaprabhu became more silent. He entered in deeper thought of Lord Sri Krishna and spent all the time in Meditation, Kirtan, Dance with the songs for Lord Sri Krishna and by listening to the reading of the Srimad Bhagawat from lifelong friend Gadadhar. Jagadananda, Swarup Damodar used to look after Mahaprabhu all the time. Govinda who once served Ishwarpuri was also engaged himself to serve Him.

Mahaprabhu Sri Chaitanyadev was always in the world of Lord Sri Krishna and Radharani. He saw the water of Sea as water of Jamuna where Lord Sri Krishna and Radharani with other companions are playing. Seeing the Chatak hill He runs towards it seeing it as the Gobardhan Hill where Lord Sri Krishna saved the people of Braja from Indra's red eye, devastating and incessant rains for seven days showered by Indra.

Seeing the garden full of beautiful small trees with nice

and fragranant flowers Mahaprabhu takes it as Vrindavan where Lord Sri Krishna and Radharani are playing all the time with Lalita, Bishakha and other Sakhis and Manjaris who are always attending at Their services. Mahaprabhu's such condition that can hardly be explained.

Mahaprabhu Sri Chaitanyadev's madly condition may only be compared with the condition of madness of Braja Gopis and Sri Radhika in Vrindavan when they saw once Uddhav and once Narada in Braja only. Nobody can resist Him from madly quest for Sri RadhaKrishna and the places of the Eternal Lila.

One day having escaped the eyes of others He being thoroughly engrossed in Love for The eternal Love of Sri Radhakrishna dived into the water of the sea considering it the Yamuna of Vrindavan. The waves of the sea took Him away. All who were present in Puri being spread and divided in several teams started to search Him in the Temple of Jagannath, Temple at Gundicha, at Narendra, at Chatak hill, at Konark, at Seashore and at places of every possible corner. Being disappointed at every place suddenly one group of searching teams found a fisherman was running, dancing and singing loudly 'Hare Krishna' repeatedly. They stopped him on his way and knew that a man like a lump of gold has been caught in his net instead of a big fish. By touching the body he found that the Golden lump was breathing slowly but after that he has been possessed by spirit. They took the fisherman and ran to the place where the Golden Mahaprabhu was lying on sands. They sang the name of Lord Sri Krishna loudly and after sometime Mahaprabhu opened His eyes. He described that He noticed Lord Sri Krishna is playing with Radhika and other Gopis in the water of Kalindi and so, He jumped into the sea to get Them all along.

Jagadananda, Swarup Damodar and Govinda remains at His door all the time so that Mahaprabhu cannot go outside without any of them.

Mahaprabhu yet in his silence mood advised His closed associates many important things including what to do's and what not to do's for the Vaishnavas. He also composed Sri Jagannath Slokastaka and Siksha Slokastaka.

The situation became that even at sleepless guarding Mahaprabhu somehow could get chance to come outside of the room and ran for Lord Sri Krishna and Radharani.

The Learning from Mahaprabhu-Love

God is Love and Love is God. Sri Krishna is the Satchidananda Bigraha Param Purusha.

Mahaprabhu Sri Chaitanyadev taught us that love to human being is the urgent part of love to God. If someone loves God, he can love others, if he can love all in the Universe he can love God. We must have the practice to love Lord Sri Krishna through our love to human being and each creation and everything in the Universe.

He has made the whole Universe. Moreover, the Universe is Himself.

Siksha Slokastaka

Perhaps Mahaprabhu had written many. But Mahaprabhu's other writings except the Siksha Slokastaka and a few Slokas are not available.

He taught thousands of His students and followers in Nabadwip and in East Bengal and millions of devotees, especially Sri Sanatan, Sri Roop and Sri Jib in Varanasi (Kashidham), Puri and in Vrindavan. Mahaprabhu Gourangadev once defeated a world conquerer scholar Keshav Kashmiri at ease during the Vidya Vilas time. Everybody of the time and till date agree that Sri Chaitanyadev was a vastly learned scholar and He had extra-ordinary intellect.

However, Siksha Slokastaka the gist of His educative advices is so far available and Sri Krishnadas Kabiraj had inserted it in the Sri Sri Chaitanya Charitamrita.

We find His Octave in poetic forms in Sanskrit that bear the essence of Goudiya Vaishnavism. That is a great scope of learning for the devotees for the future generations.

Let us cite from Sri Sri Chaitanyacharitamrita-

1. *"Chetodarpanamarjanag Bhabamahadabagni nirbapanang*
   Shreyah kairabachandrikabitaranang Vidyabadhujivanam.
   Anandambudhivardhanang pratipadang purnamritwasadaang
   Sarbatmasnapanang parang vijayatey Srikrishna sankirtanam"

That cleanses the filth from mirror like mind. That extinguishes forest-fire like heat of earthly life. What gives the moon light on Kumuda like flowers graciously. What is like a pure soul of excellently educated bride. That expands the ocean of heavenly pleasure. Whose each and every step provides the taste of juice of nector completely. What gives us complete satisfaction, that chanting of Lord Sri Krishna's name has won with all perfection.

2. *"Namnamkari bahudha nijasarbashaktistatrarpita niyamitah smaraney nah kalah*
   Etadrishi taba kripa bhagammahmapi durddaibameedri-shmihajani nanuragah."

God has expressed Himself in many names, God has rest all His powers on those names too. By memorising Him to spell His name there remains no rule. Oh Lord, such is your kindness! Alas, this is my misfortune that I have got no attachment in thy name.

3. *"Trinadapi sunichena taroriba sahishnuna*
   Amaaninamaandena kirtaniyah sada Harih."

(To become a real Vaishnav) Be lower than a single grass. Be tolerant like a tree. Give due respect to others without having hopes to earn respect. Always do chant the glory of the name of God Hari, Sri Krishna.

4. *"Na dhanang na janang na sundaring, kabitang ba Jagadisha na kamaye*
   Mamo janmani janmaniswarey, bhabatadbhaktirhaituki twayi."

Oh Lord, I do not desire wealth, do not expect people, not a beautiful wife and even I do not want the capacity of writing ornamental poems. My only prayer is that I may get the causeless devotion to thy in all my births.

5. *"Oee Nandatanuja kinkarang patitang maang bishamey bhabambudhoi*
Kripaya taba paadpankaja sthitadhuli sadrishah bichintiya."

Hello, Nanda's son Sri Krishna, I am fallen in the undulating ocean of mortal life. I am yours a servant. Please treat me a smallest particle of the dust at your divine feet.

6. *"Nayanang galadashrudharaya badanang gadhgadrudhaya gira*
Pulakoinirchitang bapuh kada taba naamgrahaney bhabishyati."

Oh Lord, such a day when would come as my eyes would be filled with melted stream of tears at the time when I shall utter your Divine Name. When my mouth would be chocked with the words of praising You with excessive emotion and my body would be thrilled with unlimited pleasure.

7. *"Yugaitang nimishena..chakshusha prabrishayitam Sunyaitang jagat sarbang Gobindabiharena mey."*

With the separation from Govinda a single moment appears to me a longer age. My eyes have been drenched as in rains and the world seems to be vacant.

8. *"Aashlishya ba padaratang pinastumumadarsananmar-mahatang karotuba*
Yatha tatha ba biddhatu lampato, matprannaathstu sa eba naaparah."

(He is Lord Sri Krishna) I am the servant at His divine eternal feet and He may, if He desires so, crush me by embracing on His chest. He may hurt me by not giving a single stare on me. Or He being a polygamist may take pleasure anywhere as per His choice. Yet, He is the beloved one of mine, the only one, none else.

Raganuga Devotion (in short)

Mahaprabhu always remained in Raganuga devotion. In the process of Sadhana of Braja Prem, Raganuga is the best of all the ways of Devotion of Lord Sri Krishna and Radharani, the Eternal Twined in bliss.

Nothing to demand or expect from Lord Sri Krishna but to worship Him as Radharani worshipped. She feels happiness on Sri Krishna's happiness and the Brojo Gopis find themselves at the service of Radharani. The eternal servants and manjoris of Radharani get unlimited pleasure with the happiness of the eternal Yugal Lord Sri Radhakrishna. Only allegiance to Radharani as well as Sri Krishna without aspiring anything in return as a manjori servant is Mahaprabhu's theme of Raganuga Sadhana.

HOMAGE

We must pay our heartiest homage to Lord Sri Chaitanyadev and His lifetime associate Sri Gadadhar Pundit. In the month of Ashara at Saptami of full moon Sunday in the evening Mahaprabhu with tears in eyes for extreme Love for God Lord Jagannath, entered into the Temple at Gundicha wherein Prabhu Jagannathdev has been placed after Rathayatra. He told Gadadhar Pundit to remain outside the Temple but Gadadhar knew after waiting half an hour that Mahaprabhu has emerged into Deity of Lord Jagannath and Gadadhar rushed into that Temple to find Mahaprabhu and he also did not back from the Temple.

Krishnadas Kabiraj in the Sri Sri Chaitanyacharitamrita did not prefer to mention any of the actual happenings whatever it were. He just wrote—

"Prabhur Ananta Lila Naa Pari Bujhitey,
Buddhi-Prabesh nahi tatey Naa pari Barnitey,
Sob Shrota Vaishnaver Bandiya Charan,
Chaitanya Charit barnan Koila Samapan."

The elderly scholar with lot of knowledge and experiences paid his last salute by bending his head to the readers only and concluded the writing Sri Sri Chaitanyacharitamrita.

However, Sri Vrindavandas in the Sri Chaitnya Bhagawat had written—

"Gaoadharey Boley Prabhu - Shuno Gadadhar,
Aami Aage Jaai Tumi Aashaha Paschatey,"- Mahaprabhu told Gadadhar to listen to Him that He is entering and Gadadhar to enter afterwards.

....

"Gadadhar Jaanilen - Prabhura Gaman,
Prabhur Birahey Tan Na Rahey Jiban,
Achambite Gadadhar Hoila Antardhan,
Naa Paay Dekhitey Keho Boley - Ramah."

A few minutes later Gadadhar Pundit knew that Mahaprabhu has gone and so Gadadhar cannot live without Mahaprabhu any longer. Suddenly Gadadhar disappeared.

...

"Eaimotey Mahaprabhu Gadadhar Loiah,

Nijasthaney Gela Prabhu Antardhan Hoiah,"- Thus Mahaprabhu taking Gadadhar disappeared and went to His own place.

It is also hearsay that Swarup Damodar was found dead after bleeding from heart on the road outside the Gundicha Temple.

We believe the spiritual thoughts and consciousness of Lord Sri Chaitanyadeva with His life long associate Gadadhar Pundit and others are deathless.

Gadadhar Pundit's life was completely mixed with the life of Lord Sri Chaitanyadev and so we bow our heads to them all for the years passed and for the years yet to come in future. May They both Lord Radhakrishna be with us.

Please pardon the writer if anything written found wrong from the information made available here and there.

May God bless you all and please pray a bit to Him for the author.

Radhakrishna Goswami (Radhu Goswami)

ON LORD SRI CHAITANYADEV

Lalon Faquir

(17/10/1774 -17/10/1890 ref. Sansad Bangalee Charitabhidhan p. 500)

Lalon Faquir was a poet and Boul singer (the first Boul as known) and he was highly respected by all of the both sides of Bengal. Rabindranath Tagore was also inspired with his songs. In one of his songs he wrote—...O taar nei jeter rog. eman paagal ke dekhechhe.." who has seen such a man who has no disease of casteism. Again—what nonsense we boast of our clan and birth... Gourahari was a kool's kool—the end of embark who drove the casteism.

Sri Ramakrishna Paramahansadev (18/02/1836—16/08/1886 A.D.)

Sri Ramakrishnadev sometime used to become overwhelmed and almost fainted in love for God by chanting or listening to Kirtan on Lord Sri Krishna and on the Holy life or Sri Chaitanyadev. He escalated the movement of Sri Gouranga Mahaprabhu giving proper respect to all human beings including all creations of God.

Once Sri Ramakrishna expressed that if a drop of love that Sri Chaitanyadev had for Lord people would get unlimited divine peace. The love for God was more than complete satisfaction. His profound attraction and insanity for God cannot be compared with anything in the world. (Sri Ramakrishna Kathamrita by Srimo 1/10/3).

Rishi Bankimchandra Chatterjee (26/06/1838 - 8/04/1894)

The writer of the national songs Vandemataram, Rishi Bankimchandra Chattopadhyay was the most pioneer of modern Bengali Literature once wrote—"It is heard from History that people of in bondage do not feel enthusiasm in expressing themselves in Culture, Literature etc. Yet, Vidyapati, Chandidas were born in this period. Thereafter in Nabadwip the Moon Sri Chaitanya was appeared. Then Roop, Sanatan and other Poets and Scholars (Pundits) were born. In the other side Raghunath Siromani, Gadadhar Pundit, Jagadish, Raghunandan and many others came forward. Again a tidal weave was experienced in the field of Bengali Poems. (Bangalar Etihaas o Chaitanyachandrodayaya)

Navin Chandra Sen (1847-1909)

Once the poet of pre -Rabindranath wrote in a poem—

..."Dui paarshey Nityananda Gadadhar paritey
aabeshe rakhichhen dhari,
Kakhano bhutaley parhiya aabeshey sonar putul
jaay garagori".

Here the poet expressed the situation of Mahaprabhu Sri Chaitanya's chanting with love for Sri Krishna. There remained Nityananda and Gadadhar all the time with Him. (In his 'Amritava' 10th Canto Patitodhara chapter)

Surendranath Bandyopadhaya (10/11/1848 - 6/08/ 1925)

Surendranath Banerjee was one of the pioneers of Freedom Fighters of India. He was also social reformer, wrote—At the time when Raghunandan and few others were engaged in formation of Hindu regulations and the Smriti Shahstra the greatest reformer of all the ages in India Sri Chaitanya Mahaprabhu appeared. He saw all irrespective of castes, sex, religions, regions, languages everything likewise. He had the 'Samadrishti, to everyone.... He also wanted to wipe out the rule of widowism from the society. ....He had to fight against the prevailing blindness and religious beliefs. He sometime succeeded with the strong personality and love to all. In Him the very speciality of Indian minds reflected accurately. People of India got a flood of divine light that gave them inspirations and learning to become faithful. So, Mahaprabhu was the greatest reformer of the society....". (Samaj Sanskarak Chaitanya).

Bepin Chandra Pal (7/11/1858 - 20/05/1932)

One of great Freedom Fighters and social reformer Bepin Chandra Pal wrote—"the Vaishnavism of Bengal introcued by Sri Chaitanya Mahaprabhu infused not only divine philosophy or Poetics or Sweetness in Bengali Lyrics but also taught that God remains in everything. His movement was towards the welfare of person as well as the society...Sri Chaitanya Mahaprabhu advised all to utter the name (naam) of Lord Sri Krishna only and not to discuss about others but to worship sincerely Lord Sri Krishna... There was no scope of any kind of impatience with other religion and not to combat with other philosophy in Mahaprabhu's propaganda... 'Chandalohapi dwija shrestha Haribhakti parayana'.. . ThisVaishnav idealism in caste inhabited in Brahmin society brought a revolution. .." (Banglar Vaishnavdharmey Samaj Sansakarak o Gana-aandolan)

Rabindranath Tagore (7/05/1861 - 7/08/1941)

In many writings of the great poet, Nobel Lauriet Rabindranath Tagore we find Vaishnav Philosophy, Vaishnav songs, theme of Sri Krishna, especially the eternal flute of Lord Sri Krishna. We find Vaishnav poems in Sonaar Tori and essence of Vaishnav thoughts in Manushya of Panchabhut, Bangabhasha o Sahitya, Kavi sangeet, Bangla Bhasha o Bangalee, Shantiniketan, Pather Sanchaya, Chaaritra Puja, in some letters to Kadambini Devi and to Hemantabala.

We find also the character Gora the name of the character who mainly wanted at last the religion of leaving aside all the differences among the Mankind a slight reflection in the novel Gora after almost 400 years of Sri Chaitanya.

His all the songs known as Rabindra Sangeet are addressed to the Almighty the Brahma or Lord Sri Krishna.

In the Nobel awarded Gitanjali, love and complete surrender to God Sri Krishna touched the theme of Lord

Sri Chaitanya propagated in Vaishnavism. Rabindranath Tagore had a deep attraction towards such feeling that Sri Chaitanya spread in Bengal, Orissa and rest of the Country. He confessed that, "with the advent of Vaishnav movement all the birds all on a sudden as if woke up and started to sing with melodious voices. From this we can guess that Bengal could feel herself appropriately in the Vaishnav movement". (Sahitya)

Swami Vivekananda (12/01/1863 - 4/07/1902)

Swami Vivekananda disciple of Sri Ramakrishna propagated the glory of Hinduism in World Conference at Chicago in 1993 and all the philosophers of all the religions of the world were surprised to note it.

Once he wrote "...Among all the incarnations Mahaprabhu Chaitanya was the best". (Avatara Baristha-Complete Works-Centenary Volume).

He wrote : "...there exits the influence of Sri Chaitanya in the whole of India. Wherever Bhakti prevails people chant and worship of Him and discuss His Lila..." (Complete Works-Volume IV)

In the reply to the Reception Ceremony in Madras (now renamed as Chennai) he referred as,"... Once the noble talent tore the prolonged nets of oppression and stood erect - it is Bhagwan Sri Krishnachaitanya.." (Sahitya Mela-June 1986)

He wrote that, ".. Such a divine exposure as seen in Nadiavatara Sri Krishna Chaitanya that cannot be seen anywhere..." (C.W. Vol. V)

Dinesh Chandra Sen (3/11/1866 -20/11/1939)

Dinesh Chandra Sen was an eminent historian, scholar and a lifelong research personality. He traveled remote villages and collected many old scriptures, books etc. and introduced systematic researches of Bengali literature. "Bangla Bhasha O Sahitya" is one of the fruits of his hard labour. He was appointed and honoured with the post, newly introduced, of reader from 1909-13 and awarded with the Ramtanu Lahiri Research Fellowship in the University of Calcutta. He received D.Lit. in 1921 and Jagattarini Gold Award in 1931 from the Calcutta University. His notable works are: Maimansingha Geetika O Sahitya Parichaya, Bengali Ramayana, Ramayani Katha, Behula, Sati, Fullara, The Vaishnav Literature of Mediaval Bengal, Chaitanya and His Companions, Chaitanya and His Age, Brihad Banga etc. He wrote in his essay Vaishnav Padabali O Sri Chaitanya-"...Gourhari established the truthfulness of Srimad Bhagawat and Vaishnav Geetis. He has shown the vast enormous scriptures are based on Bhakti, tears and love. Love for Lord Sri Krishna. Purba Raag (Amorous attraction/ courtship) separation, meeting, all these flowing are not as imaginary story. All these were testable and were tasted. Sri Gour became a divine tree of kadamba with the splendid pleasure. Sea waves became the waves of Yamuna, Chatak hill became the Gobardhan, and the whole world became full of Lord Sri Krishna.

Deshabandhu Chittaranjan Das (5/11/1870 - 16/06/1925)

Deshabandhu Chittaranjan Das was popular in the

name of C.R. Das in the history of Freedom Struggle of India and of the National Congress Party. Before coming in the Independence Movement he was a renowned poet at his time and he edited a periodical entitled Narayan. He was a famous Bar-at-Law and out of many important cases he pleaded for Sri Aurobindo Ghosh against the British Empire.

Once he wrote—"...Gouranga's divine appearance turned my lifestyle....Sri Krishna Chaitanya's beauty beyond imagination, His solemn divine voice, the control on superhuman talents, possessing incomparable love for God in the heart brought deluge in the society and it flooded the whole Country. Bengal then was full of resoundings of Mridanga like the roars of clouds of rains and with the chanting of Harinaam ... ."(Banglaar Geeti Kavita O Sri Krishna Chaitanya)

In the Presidential speech in 1917 at Bhowanipore (Kolkata) at the Bengal Province conference—"...We were overflooded with the Swadeshi Movement and with this flood as if we are survived and could feel our living soul and got it.....In the stream of Bengal's History we have experienced Bouddha's Buddha, Shiva Mahadeva of the child stage, strength of the Saktas and unconditional devotion of Vaishnavas. We listened to songs of Chandidas-Vidyapati. The glory of divinity of Mahaprabhu enhanced our glory".

Sri Aurobindo (Aurovinda Ghosh) (15/08/1872 - 5/12/1950)

Sri Aurobindo (Aurovinda Ghosh) is considered as the Rishi of modern age. Sri Aurobindo's main inspiration was

Lord Sri Krishna. He found Him in the jail at Alipore. So, he had special likings for Sri Chaitanya. In his writing 'The Demand of the Mother' in the Bandemataram on April 11,1908 expressed..."The perfect sense of self-abandonement which Chaitanya felt for Hari must be felt by Bengal for the Mother... our passion to see the face or free and glorified Mother must be as devouring a madness as the passion of Chaitanya to see the face of Sri Krishna."

He also commented—"...In Chaitanya sometimes the Incarnation of Sri Krishna was observed. This divine expression was worth mentioning.....Chaitanyadev placed the Radhafeelings at the highest place because in the divine thoughts the place of complete pleasure is on the highest position same as the Upanishdas that express the feeling of extreme pleasure is on the highest position.

Chakravarti T. Rajagopalachari (1879-1972)

Rajagopalachari known as Rajaji was the first and last Governor-General of India (1948-50), Chief Minister of Madras, Home Minister in the Nehru's Cabinet and Governor of West Bengal and recipient of Bharat Ratna (1954). He commented in The Vạisnavite Reformers of India—"...Whatever may be the truth about Chaitanya's Divinity, it is clear that he was, in actual life, Sri Krishna for the 16th century."

Panchkodi Bandyopadhayay (20/12/1886- 15/11/1923)

An essayist and a renowned literateur of the last century having books like Banglaar Samajik Etihaas, translations and editing of Aein-E-Akbar and the life of Akbar, Sri Chaitanyacharitamrita, Roop Laharee O Rooper Katha etc. He knew Hindi, Urdu, Farshi, English and some other languages. He had lot of research works in his credit. In his Bhubanantak Gadadhar' sub-chapter of his important essay Bangalir Bishistata he wrote—"Gadadhar Pundit was an incomparable Pundit in Logics during the period of Sri Chaitanya. In his hereditary till 1890, upto Bhuban Chandra Vidyaratna the family topped the list of pundits of Logics. (Banga Darpan-W.B. Govt. Higher Education Council)

Dr. Sarvepalli Radhakrishnan (5/09/1888 - 17/04/1975)

Dr. Sarvepalli Radhakrishnan is an Indian scholar, philosopher, writer and statesman. He was the first Vice-President (1952-62) and the second President (1962-67) of India. Formerly, he was a professor at Oxford and the Chairman of UNESCO. He received Bharat Ratna award in 1954, Templeton award in 1975. In one of his famous writings 'Indian Philosophy' he commented that the four pioneers of Indian religion Buddhadev, Nagarjun, Sankaracharya and Sri Chaitanya are the great thinkers; the others are mere scholars.

Dr. Ramesh Chandra Majumdar (4/12/1888 - 12/02/1980)

Dr. Ramesh Chandra Majumdar a renowned Historian and Writers of Books like, Corporate Life in Ancient India, Outline of ancient Indian History and Civilisation, The Sepoi Mutiny and revolt of 1857, History of Freedom,

Bangadesher Etihaas etc. wrote in his writing Mahaprabhu Sri Chaitanya—"Adwyaitacharya was shocked to find the citizens without devotion to Lord Sri Krishna. Sri Chaitanyadev was successful to ease his sorrow.....love for no reason to Lord Sri Krishna can be expressed through Shantya, Dasya, Sakhya, Batsalya and Madhuryya. The symbol of Madhuryya is the love of Radha and the Gopis to Sri Krishna. This love is Divine and beyond human body. This was the novel Vaishnav religion that was, introduced in Bengal by Sri Chaitanyadev....His strong manliness, real purity and uncommon and rare personality uplifted the Vaishnav religion to higher standard than it was in practice."

Kazi Nazrul Islam (25/05/1898 - 29/08/1976)

Kazi Nazrul Islam one of the most preferred poets of Bengal fought against British Imperialism with his poems and songs full of lyrics and melodies based on Ragas. Many of his poems and songs carried bravery against all kinds of ill forces specially tyrannies, oppressions, bondage and were full of feelings of brotherhood, unity national as well as international, devotion to God irrespective of beliefs and above all humanity. He loved Sri Chaitanya also. In one of his songs on Lord Gouranga he described Mahaprabhu Gouranga a united soul of Radha and Krishna—"...Kende se Krishner prem bhiksha maage dwarey dwarey....".

APPENDIX

Panchatattwa

Bhaktarup Sri Gouranga, Bhaktasrirup Sri Nityananda, Bhaktabatar Sri Adwyaita, Bhakta Sri Sribaas and Bhaktashakti Sri Gadadhar.

Six Goswami

Sri Sanatan, Sri Roop, Sri Raghunath Bhatta, Sri Gopal Bhatta, Srijib and Sri Raghunathdas, and other two Goswami Sri Bhugarva and Sri Lokenath.

Six Chakraborty

Sri Vyas, Sridam, Sri Gokulananda, Sri Shyamadas, Sri Govinda (Bhaabak Chakraborty) and Sri Ramcharan.

Eight Kaviraj

Sri Ramchandra, Sri Govinda, Sri Karnapur, Sri Nrisingha, Sri Bhagawan, Sri Ballavikanta, Sri Gopiraman and Sri Gokul.

Twelve Gopal

All Sri - Abhiram Thakur, Uddharan Dutta, Kamalakr Piplai, Kala Krishnadas, Gouridas Pundit, Dhananjoy Pundit, Parameswari Das, Nagar Purusottam, Purusottam Das, Mahesh Pundit, Sridhar (banana conch seller) and Sundarananda Thakur.

Thakur, Banamali Das, Srikar Pundit, Srinidhi Pundit, Lakshman Acharya and Purshottam Pundit.

Sri Sen Sibananda

Sri Makaraddhwaj Dutta, Raghunath Dutta, Madhu Pundit, Bishnudas Acharya, Purandar Mishra, Gobindo Thakur, Paramananda Gupta and Balaram Das.

Sri Gobinda Ghosh

Kashi Mishra, Sikhi Mahati, Sriram Pundit, Baro Haridas (Brihat Haridas or Kalidas), Kabi Chandra, Hiranya Garbha and Dwija Pitambar.

Sri Madhab Ghose (or Bakreswar Pundit)

Makaraddhwaj Sen, Vidya Bachaspati, Gobindo Acharya, Mahesh Thakur, Srikanta, Madhab Pundit, Sadananda Saraswati and Balabhadra Bhattacharya.

Sri Basudev Ghosh

Madhav Pundit, Murari Chaitanya Das, Makaraddhwaj Pundit, Kongshari Sen, Srijib Pundit, Mukunda Kabiraj, Choto Haridas and Kobi Chandra Gupta.

(Ref: Banglaar Kirtan O Kirtaniya by Harekrishna Mukhopadhyay, a publication from Govt. of W. Bengal State Book Board).

Index